MARRIAGE AND FAMILY LAW IN
BRITISH COLUMBIA

MARRIAGE AND FAMILY LAW IN BRITISH COLUMBIA

The rights of husbands, wives, children, and common-law spouses

Jane Auxier, LL.B.
Karen Nordlinger, Q.C.

Self-Counsel Press

(*a division of*)
International Self-Counsel Press Ltd.
Vancouver
Toronto   Seattle

Printed in Canada

First edition: November, 1972
Second edition: June, 1974; Reprinted: June, 1977
Third edition: May, 1980
Fourth edition: August, 1981
Fifth edition: December, 1982
Sixth edition: April, 1985
Seventh edition: March, 1989

Canadian Cataloguing in Publication Data
Auxier, Jane.
    Marriage and family law in British Columbia
      (Self-counsel series)
      Previously published: B.C. family law and guide
to drafting marriage contracts / by R. Flynn Marr.
      ISBN 0-88908-434-3

1. Domestic relations — British Columbia — Popular works.
2. Marriage law — British Columbia — Popular works.
3. Parent and child (Law) — British Columbia — Popular works.
I. Nordlinger, Karen F.   II. Title.   III. Series.
KEB 194.Z82M37 1989 346.71101'5 C89-091076-6

Self-Counsel Press
(a division of)
International Self-Counsel Press Ltd.
1481 Charlotte Road
North Vancouver, British Columbia V7J 1H1

CONTENTS

LIST OF SAMPLES

NOTICE TO READERS

Laws are constantly changing. Every effort is made to keep this publication as current as possible. However, neither the authors nor the publisher can accept any responsibility for changes to the law or practice that occur after the printing of this publication. Please be sure that you have the most recent edition.

INTRODUCTION

In recent years our western culture has changed its emphasis from a sacrosanct preservation of the family as a unit to the individual independence of the members of the family.

The ease of obtaining a divorce (in comparison with the situation before 1968), the relaxation of stringent codes of sexual morality, the new status of women in society — all of these factors have caused both men and women to examine their roles as spouses more carefully and to sever the relationship in the family unit when circumstances demand it. Twenty years ago divorce was a stigma and problems in a marriage had to be tolerated; today divorce is acceptable, and problems of a serious and insoluble nature frequently result in the disruption of the family unit.

It is unfortunate that, despite our rapidly expanding sources of communication, many individuals are unaware of the rights and obligations that arise from the separation of a husband and wife. A wife may have contemplated separation or even divorce, but has hesitated because her husband has threatened to "cut her off without a cent." A husband may have contemplated leaving his wife, but has hesitated because his wife has threatened to "take him for every penny he has" or to "make certain that he never sees the children again." It is on rare occasions that threats of this nature have any validity in law.

The purpose of this book is to acquaint you in general terms with the nature of a marriage and the consequences of a separation. If you have serious matrimonial problems, you should consult a lawyers.

1

HUSBAND AND WIFE

a. WHAT IS A MARRIAGE — LEGALLY AND OTHERWISE?

During the last few thousand years of our cultural history, marriage and the extended family has been the basis of our social structure. ("Extended family" refers to the older family structure in which several generations and their relations by marriage either lived in the same dwelling or resided close enough to each other to still be considered one family unit.) And because these institutions have been entrusted with the care and raising of the children of our community, the state has always had a vested interest in every marriage and, for that matter, any other situation in which children are being reared, for the children are the one product on which the whole community depends for its existence.

Since before Roman times, this institution has been a matter of contract, at first between families, and later between the parties themselves. As time passed, the form picked up certain religious trappings, then state sanction, and, finally, today it comes to us encrusted and hoary with centuries tangled in its hair. But it is still basically considered a contract, not in the usually accepted sense possibly, but similar enough in form to be classed under that broad head of jurisprudence.

One legal writer has said,

> I have throughout treated marriage as a contract, because this is the light in which it is ordinarily viewed by jurists, domestic and

1

foreign. But it appears to me to be something more than a mere contract. It is rather to be deemed an institution of society founded upon the consent and contract of the parties; and in this view it has some peculiarities in its nature, character, operation and extent of obligation, different from what belongs to an ordinary contract.

Once two people are married, the law takes on for them certain new aspects. Certain legal obligations arise between the parties themselves and between the parties and society as a whole. And, depending on whether or not these two people have entered into a legal marriage or what is commonly called a common-law marriage, society has a say in determining the type of relationship the parties will have.

The noble old institution does have its problems. For example, the law was never very precise about who does what in marriage, and does not provide a remedy when the parties are in dispute about how the marriage itself is to work. Years ago the problem was somewhat controlled because women really had no alternatives to consider. This is not the case today with so many women in the workforce. The alternatives are now present, and both men and women are questioning their roles in marriage. In fact, many young people are questioning the whole institution.

The large extended family has disappeared and now we find the nuclear family, mom and dad, trying to do all of the tasks that once many hands pitched in to do. It is a heavy burden, and it tears at the resolve of the individuals involved. And with the mobility of our population we find people alone, away from the family, isolated and cut off in a world that can be very hostile. The challenges from without tend to disrupt within. With the liberation of wife, the growing arrogance of children, the hard-sell good life thrown at dad, and a thousand other diversions, it is sometimes hard to keep

2

clear the goals and the paths to those goals. All of these problems combined add up to a great pressure on every marriage relationship — so much so that we can well wonder what its future may be.

When two people do marry, the contract that they enter into is defined for them by law. They can also enter into a separate contract that sets out further principles — the so-called "marriage contract" — and this is discussed in another part of this book.

When two people enter into a common-law relationship, there are also certain principles of contract involved, although far fewer, and the obligations that common-law spouses incur toward each other tend to arise more directly from the provisions of the Family Relations Act. Rights and remedies between common-law partners tend to be a little more complex and are more likely to require the assistance of a lawyer should the relationship break down and require sorting out in the courts.

One form of union that is often discussed is a homosexual one: a relationship between two persons of the same sex. In law, this concept violates the very definition of marriage, and any contract entered into for that purpose would very likely be unenforceable before the courts which refuse to enforce any agreement that is in violation of or contrary to "public policy."

However, as we shall see, such a contract would have value in a non-legal sense, in that the parties concerned would take the time to consider the nature and obligations of the relationship into which they are entering. If, in the future, a struggle developed over property or other civil matters, a court trying to settle a dispute between such persons might well look to an agreement that the parties had entered into earlier to determine their intentions. And, of course, the same comments would apply for group marriages and all other permutations and combinations of man and woman that do not have the usual historical sanction.

b. DIFFERENCES BETWEEN FORMAL AND COMMON-LAW MARRIAGES

Once, long ago, marriage was not public in that it did not involve church or government. It was something composed wholly of tradition and the people: in other words, it was civil in nature. From about the 10th century on, the church became more and more involved, but valid marriages could still be entered into by contract as in the old way. The situation became chaotic as young people went off privately and, without telling mom and dad, formed valid marriages in secret. Eventually, about 1750 A.D., the government in England stepped in and passed a Marriage Act that set out how valid marriages were to be entered into.

The law in British Columbia does not sanction marriages not performed according to the provisions of the Marriage Act, but, of course, it does not prevent people from simply living together in the old way and so there have come to be "common-law marriages." These unions have for years been outside of the law, and as the law of the family began to grow in the 19th century, the common-law union was ignored and the protections and benefits of marriage were not conferred upon it.

In Canada, and particularly in British Columbia, common-law marriage has received little recognition until recently. However, as more and more people in our society choose to live in this type of relationship, the legislature has begun to realize that these people also require the protection of the law.

The basic difference then between formal marriage and the common-law relationships, has been that the parties in the former have legal status and a wide variety of rights and obligations, while those in the latter have very limited rights and obligations. A common-law relationship allows for more freedom and flexibility, and one partner has very little control over the other. Many people feel that it is' not right for one person to have "control" over another, especially if the partners are equal.

Problems arise when the parties are not equal — when one partner has more training and skill than the other and is better able to find a good job, or when one partner is charged with the bulk of the obligation and emotional strain of raising children.

Recent changes in the law concerning common-law relationships indicate recognition of the reliance that common-law spouses place on one another in some circumstances. However, the government has chosen not to give full recognition to such unions, probably because the legal situation would become entangled and chaotic if the briefest liaison between a couple was vested with all the rights of the matrimonial relationship. Government still wishes to encourage couples to marry and has, therefore, ensured that marriage carries with it many more rights and obligations. When couples marry they generally wish to enter into a closer bond with one another.

Status between people formally married is fixed and covered by a legal framework of rules, rights, and obligations. It is very different from any other type of relationship. To qualify for protection, a spouse need only produce a certified copy of the marriage certificate which can be had for $15. No fuss, no muss, no bother.

In human relationships, however, it is difficult to be protected from a bitter person. When a union (formal or informal) is on the rocks, it can get rough and one person may have difficulty dealing with the other. It is unfortunate that even the most idealistic of relationships can break up and it is at this juncture that the issue of marriage or common-law marriage becomes extremely important.

The main advantage of living common-law is that the relationship can end without the interference of the courts; a married couple must obtain a divorce which is frequently unpleasant and necessitates, for most, the services of a lawyer. From a purely practical point of view, the woman's position is usually worse than her ex-husband's. Without the earning power of her mate, and often with the prime responsibility for the children, she is on the bottom and her struggle is an uphill one and, in many cases, an unfair one. But there are always ways to equalize the imbalance, which we discuss in this book.

c. THE FORMALITIES OF ENGAGEMENT AND MARRIAGE

The formalities of marriage in this province are governed by the Marriage Act. As already pointed out, this statute sets out the terms and conditions under which two people may marry and is very similar in form to the original Marriage Act passed in England about 1750.

Engagement is governed by the "common law." (The common law is age old custom that has grown into formal law by being forged piece by piece in one reported legal decision after another.) Basically, an engagement is a contract to marry and is governed by the ordinary rules of contract. If one person breaks the contract, it may be possible to recover damages if the other can prove that damages were suffered as a result of the breach. This used to be a very popular form of action but is not often used now. Consult a lawyer if you intend to take this step as it is fairly complex.

As has already been mentioned, a marriage is a form of contract with certain implied terms conditional to it. Of these terms there are very few that the parties themselves can alter by their own will and desire. The formalities of the marriage as set out in the Marriage Act must be strictly observed. Basically the Marriage Act sets out two ways in which the marriage contract can be concluded. One involves the church and religious ceremonies and the other is by way of marriage licence and civil ceremony.

Complications arise when very young people desire to marry. Under the age of 19, both persons require the consent of their parents, and should the parents not consent, the young couple may apply to a Supreme Court judge for consent. Under the age of 16, the consent of all parents is required together with the consent of the Supreme Court judge. It is interesting to note, however, that once the marriage has been performed and the marriage has been consummated even though the parties are too young, it may be a valid marriage. This would mean, for instance, that if you and your spouse are under 16 years of age, and you could complete the proper form of marriage and then consummate it, you would then be validly married.

Basically, the Marriage Act states the requirements for the registration of members of the clergy who may perform marriages and states the necessity for things such as marriage licences, witnesses to the marriage, and marriage certificates. No particular formal ceremony is described in the act and provision is made for both civil and religious ceremonies. In either case, the parties to the marriage are free to write their own ceremony if they can obtain the co-operation of the presiding minister or marriage commissioner.

d. WRITTEN MARRIAGE CONTRACTS

When two people say, "I do," they are in fact saying that they agree to abide by the terms of a contract written for them in law, for better or for worse, and whether or not they like it. Regrettably, the majority of people are not even aware of the existence or the contents of this agreement in law and very often find that some of the terms of this contract — either included or excluded — are so offensive to them that, had they known, they might have chosen not to marry.

In addition, when most people marry they are doing so with many assumptions about the nature of the relationship to which their partners may not subscribe. It is unfortunate that few people seem to sit down in advance and work all of these things out on paper. Apparently love does not question, which may be the reason that love is doing so poorly these days as a foundation for a marriage. It refuses to protect itself.

1. What kind of contract can you have?

Written contracts of marriage were once very common in England. This was especially so before the existence of the Married Woman's Property Act of the last century in England that gave women basic property and contractual rights they did not have before. Since the enactment of these statutes in England, and a similar statute, the Married Woman's Property Act, in various provinces in Canada, marriage contracts fell into disuse, although they were still possible in law as long as they provided for the division of property during the marriage or upon death. Any provisions relating to separation or divorce of the parties would not be enforced because such contracts offended public policy. Certain limitations were placed on these contracts.

These limits come about because any marriage contract is really a three-cornered affair between the man, the woman, and the society, which imposes many of its own terms and conditions. To attempt to contract in any way so as to infringe upon these imposed terms and conditions would result in the courts striking down the offending provisions as being against public policy. Things such as children, sex, permanence, and monogamy, are all imposed terms.

Any attempts to contract, for example, that there be no children, that the parties remain celibate, that the marriage terminate after so many years, that there be more than one man and one woman in the relationship, or that there be any grouping of the sexes other than one of each kind would certainly be struck down in court. It is open to you to contract in any of these matters, but the courts would simply not assist you to support such a contract.

Since the introduction in British Columbia of the Family Relations Act, marriage contracts are undergoing a revival. The act embodies the concept of deferred community property: the idea that upon separation or divorce the parties will share equally in any property ordinarily used for a family purpose. The act does, however, allow you to contract out of this arrangement.

Under Section 48 of the Family Relations Act, a couple may enter into an agreement, either before or during their marriage in which they sort out the management of the family assets or other property during their marriage and determine the ownership in, or division of, family assets or other property during their marriage or in the event of separation or divorce.

Apart from these matters, which are specifically mentioned in the legislation, a marriage contract may include items such as who is to perform the household chores, which parent is to have custody of the children in the event of a separation, what the support obligations will be, and so on. It is important to realize that not all of these provisions would be enforceable by the court. For example, the courts in British Columbia have always felt that they are the overseers of the welfare of children and their jurisdiction cannot be ousted by private counsel. Therefore, the terms of custody arrangements are set by the courts. Provisions for support are also not enforceable in a court if the amount set forth in the contract does not appear reasonable in light of respective incomes and expenses.

There is still great value to including provisions that could not normally be directly enforced by the court. Parties to a marriage seldom sit down and discuss how they expect the marriage to be conducted and how they see the responsibilities being divided. With more and more women entering the workforce, more and more husbands have to face the task of sharing domestic duties. When things like cooking, house care, washing, window cleaning, and child care are all worked out in advance and set down on paper, there is a considerable psychological benefit.

First, you each get to know the other's views on these topics and have a chance to compare your spouse's views on marriage with your own. Second, when problems arise later on, the paper setting out the deal could carry great weight between you. And, finally, even though unenforceable directly, if you do end up in court in some dispute or other, the judge will be most interested in the agreement as an expression of the intentions of each of you.

Sample #1 shows an example of a pre-marriage contract and Sample #2 illustrates a marriage contract. The forms are not meant to be followed word for word. Rather they are suggestions of what the agreement might say and look like. For each couple the terms will be different, reflecting the reality of the relationship the two people foresee. As an aid in drawing up such a contract yourself, a package of pre-printed forms, *If You Love Me Put It In Writing*, is available from the publisher.

Should your intended spouse not wish to sign such a contract or come to any agreement about the intended relationship, you might consider whether or not you wish to go any further. Better the embarrassment of ending it now than the expense and heartache of legal action later. People who will not commit themselves to paper are not likely to commit themselves to you. And don't forget although the relationship you have now will mature and change as you grow older, the chances of its maturing in the direction of an increasing commitment to helping and understanding one another are not very great. Before the marriage, you are at the height of co-operation; you may expect it to grow more remote in the future. If it is unsatisfactory now, bail out.

2. The mechanics of writing a contract

All legal agreements have basically the same form, and once the form is mastered, any person can draw an agreement that could be very useful, if not completely binding, on the parties that signed it. Basically, the document must encompass on its face the whole of the agreement entered into. This is because of the existence of a rule of law that pops up every now and then and states that a formal agreement becomes the whole agreement, unless it expressly says otherwise, and that any oral details that were agreed on and not included in the agreement go by the boards.

The agreement must show the date and place that it was written, the full names and addresses of the parties who signed it, and the terms and conditions set out in it. No legal language is necessary, but the words must be clear, precise, and have only one meaning so as to avoid possible future confusion. It must be signed by all of the parties it is to bind and should be witnessed. Witnesses should insert their full names, addresses, and occupations when signing the document.

These instructions are basic, crude, and approximate. If they cannot be followed, you should not necessarily give up on the agreement. Any written memorandum signed by both parties is of value or potential value in court. Conform as closely as you can, but get it on paper and have it signed. Even the very exercise of thinking it out will be of value in the long run.

The contracts shown in Samples #1 and #2 may have limited applications in court. In your life, it may be a good investment of a few hours of time to think out what it is that you, in fact, intend to do in the future. Spend time on your contract so that your final product reflects what you want, but try to follow the form and the brief instructions for completing it as closely as possible.

The agreements are short and tend to stay away from sweeping policy and philosophical statements. Such provisions would only confuse the document should it ever have to be interpreted by a court. But, expand as you will on the examples, keeping the wording simple, in point form, and understandable.

Make enough copies of any agreement so that each of you can have a signed copy for your own records. Keep your signed copy in a safe place, even away from your spouse, so that you are certain that at least one copy will survive.

Having said all that, we should warn you that the courts are far less likely to enforce a contract when the parties have not received independent legal advice. For that reason, it might be preferable to thrash out the terms of an agreement with your partner and draft the document but then each seek legal counsel before signing.

SAMPLE #1
PRE-MARRIAGE CONTRACT

THIS AGREEMENT made in quadruplicate this 2nd day of June, 19-.

BETWEEN:

> BETTY BLISS of the City of Vancouver,
> Province of British Columbia
> hereinafter called "the future Wife"

—AND—

> LARRY LONELY of the City of Vancouver,
> Province of British Columbia
> hereinafter called "The future Husband"

WHEREAS the parties are about to enter into a marriage relationship to be duly solemnized under the laws of the Province of British Columbia on or about the 4th day of July, 19- in the City of Vancouver, in the Province of British Columbia;

AND WHEREAS the parties are of sound mind and body and have a clear understanding of the terms of this agreement and of the binding nature of the covenants contained herein; they freely and in good faith chose to enter into this marriage agreement and fully intend it to be legally binding upon themselves;

AND WHEREAS the parties hereto are desirous of determining their rights and duties during their marriage, upon death and in the event of marital difficulties to make such rights and obligations explicit so that fairness to all parties concerned may be facilitated;

AND WHEREAS each party is possessed of his or her own separate income and estate;

AND WHEREAS each party has been advised of the provisions and possible legal implications of the Family Relations Act, 1978, and intend this agreement to be a marriage agreement within meaning of the act.

NOW THIS INDENTURE WITNESSETH that in consideration of the promises of the marriage and the marriage itself and of the mutual covenants, agreements and undertakings herein set out, the parties hereby expressly agree as follows:

ARTICLE I

ASSETS AND LIABILITIES

1. The parties have made full disclosure to each other of all property and assets owned by each of them and of the income derived therefrom and from all other sources.

2. Each party shall during his or her lifetime keep and retain sole ownership, control and enjoyment of all property real and personal now owned or hereafter acquired by him or her free and clear of any claim by the other.

3. Notwithstanding any law or statute to the contrary, the parties hereto agree that they shall always be separate as to property.

4. The parties agree that those provisions of the Family Relations Act relating to family assets shall have no application whatever in the determination of ownership of assets of either party.

5. Neither party shall contract any debt in the name of the other, nor in any way bind the other for any debt for which either might in any way become liable. If either party shall at any time or times hereafter be called on to pay or discharge and shall in fact pay or discharge any debt or liability heretofore or hereafter incurred or contracted by the other, then, and in such case, the party making such payment, at his or her election and in addition to any other rights which she or he may have to recover same, may deduct and retain the amount which she or he shall have so paid out of any sum or sums of money then due or thereafter to become due to the other party; provided that she or he shall not pay any such debt or liability without first notifying the other party of the existence thereof and giving the other party an opportunity to pay it or dispute it.

6. The parties agree at all times hereafter each to keep indemnified the other, his or her heirs, executors, and administrators from all debts and liabilities heretofore or hereafter contracted or incurred by them, and from all actions, proceedings, claims, demands, costs, damages, and expenses whatsoever in respect of such debts and liabilities or any of them, other than such as arise under this agreement.

7. Without in any way limiting the generality of the foregoing provisions, it is the intention of the parties to cohabit on the lands and premises municipally known as 123 Wedded Way, Vancouver, British Columbia, which lands and premises are owned by the future Wife absolutely. The future Husband agrees to remise, release, and forever discharge the future Wife from any right or claim which he may hereinafter acquire whether at law or in equity or under the provisions of any statute past, present, or future to the said lands and premises.

8. The parties acknowledge that the future Wife is the sole owner of all the contents of the lands and premises municipally known as

123 Wedded Way, Vancouver, British Columbia, and the future Husband shall not now or in future make any claim whatever against them.

9. In the event that the future Wife desires to terminate the marital cohabitation, the future Husband agrees to vacate the lands and premises municipally known as 123 Wedded Way, Vancouver, British Columbia, within a reasonable time after being requested by the future Wife to do so, and thereafter the future Wife shall be entitled to have exclusive possession of the said lands and premises.

10. The parties acknowledge that the future Wife is the absolute owner of the lands and premises municipally known as Lot 123, Whistler, British Columbia, which said lands and premises shall be available for the mutual enjoyment of both parties as a recreational vacation property during the period of their cohabitation. The parties further acknowledge that the future Wife is the exclusive owner of the contents of and the equipment contained in or about the said lands and premises. The future Husband acknowledges that he has not now nor will hereafter acquire any right, title, claim, or interest therein.

11. In the event that the future Wife desires to terminate the marital cohabitation of the parties, she shall notify the future Husband and in such event the future Husband shall forthwith cease to be entitled to have the use or occupation of the said lands and premises at Lot 123, Whistler, British Columbia the contents of or the equipment contained therein and acknowledges that the future Wife shall have the right to exclusive possession thereof.

12. The future Wife acknowledges that the future Husband is absolutely entitled to the ownership of any chattels which he owned prior to the marriage and she shall not now or in the future make any claim whatever against them.

ARTICLE II

AFTER-ACQUIRED HOUSEHOLD GOODS

1. After-acquired household goods in this section includes furniture and effects used in or reasonably necessary to the running of

the home which are acquired by either party subsequent to the marriage of the parties, but does not include purely personal items or goods used mainly by one of the spouses whether owned or otherwise.

2. The parties shall at all times be entitled to the financial contributions of either to the acquisition, maintenance, or capital improvement of the said household goods.

ARTICLE III
MOTOR VEHICLE

1. The parties acknowledge that they are each the owner of a separate motor vehicle.

2. The parties are equally entitled to the rights of use of both motor vehicles during their cohabitation.

3. Notwithstanding paragraph 2 hereof, either party shall be free to dispose of or otherwise deal with the beneficial title in the motor vehicle registered in his or her own name without the consent of the other.

ARTICLE IV
FINANCIAL OBLIGATIONS

1. Except as provided in this agreement, neither party shall be obligated to make any payment or payments of any kind whatsoever, directly or indirectly, to or for the benefit of the other and each party expressly renounces any right or claim which he or she has had, has, or may hereinafter acquire whether at law or in equity or under the provisions of any statutes, past, present, or future against the property, both real and personal of the other, now owned or hereafter acquired by him or her. Each party covenants and agrees that this agreement may be pleaded as and shall constitute a full defence and answer to any such claim and each party agrees that he or she will not at any time hereafter seek, ask, demand, or require in any manner or make any claims for monies or property, real or personal of any nature for himself or herself.

2. Neither party shall be obliged to make any payment or payments of any kind whatsoever, directly or indirectly, to or for the benefit of the other, and each party expressly renounces any right or claim which she or he has had, has or may hereafter acquire whether at law or in equity or under the provisions of any statutes, past, present or future for alimony, interim alimony, support, maintenance or otherwise and each party covenants and agrees that this agreement may be pleaded as and shall constitute a full defence and answer to any such claims and each party hereby agrees that he or she will not at any time hereafter ask, seek, demand or require in any manner or make any claims for monies of any nature for or toward his or her support and maintenance. Any Order or Judgment for alimony, maintenance or support shall be null and void between the parties, and if any such claim is made notwithstanding, the parties reserve their right to dispute the claims for any sum; and if any such Order is made notwithstanding, each covenants with the other to indemnify him or her and save him or her harmless for the effects thereof.

3. The parties agree that forthwith upon their marriage they shall open a bank account in both of their names at a mutually agreeable bank or trust company. The parties agree that they shall each deposit into the said bank account in every calendar year the sum of $20 000 or such other sum as may be agreed upon by the parties from time to time provided that in any event each party's contribution to the said bank account shall be equal in any calendar year. The funds on deposit in the said bank account shall be used for day-to-day living expenses for the parties including but without limiting the generality of the foregoing, the household expenses and carrying charges for the lands and premises municipality known as 123 Wedded Way, Vancouver, British Columbia and Lot 123, Whistler, British Columbia, B.C. Medical Plan premiums, drugs, extra medical and dental care, club dues, entertainment, items of personal care, furniture replacement, appliance repairs, and vacations. The funds on deposit in the said bank account shall be held by the parties as tenants in common and each party shall have an undivided one-half interest therein.

In the event that a dispute arises between the parties as to the use or disposition of funds on deposit in the said bank account, one arbitrator shall be appointed by agreement between the parties and the issue in dispute shall be submitted to the arbitrator for determination. This paragraph will constitute a submission under The Arbitrations Act, RSBC, 1960, Chapter 14. The decision of the arbitrator shall be binding on all parties and shall not be subject to appeal.

4. If a dispute arises between the parties as to the use or disposition of funds on deposit in the said bank account, the parties shall attempt to resolve the dispute by mediation. E.L. Smith shall act as mediator. If he is unable to so act, the parties shall select an alternate mediator and, failing agreement, the future Wife shall select the mediator. The parties shall share equally the cost of mediation.

ARTICLE V
ESTATES

1. The future Wife releases and renounces all rights that she may have to the administration of the future Husband's estate in the event of the future Husband predeceasing her, and the future Wife renounces and releases the future Husband from any and all claims she has or may hereafter acquire against his estate under the Estate Administration Act or any other statutes or amendments thereto whereby a wife is or may be given a statutory claim against the estate of her husband.

2. The future Husband renounces all rights that he may have to the administration of the future Wife's estate in the event of the future Wife predeceasing him and the future Husband renounces and releases the future Wife from any claims which he may hereafter have against her estate under the Estate Administration Act or any other statutes or amendments thereto whereby a husband is or may be given a statutory claim against the estate of his wife.

ARTICLE VI
VARIATION AND TERMINATION

1. This agreement cannot be varied or terminated at any time except by written agreement of both parties.

ARTICLE VII

CONTRACTUAL UNDERSTANDING

1. The parties to this agreement, while desiring this agreement to operate both as a guideline to their marital rights and responsibilities and as a legally enforceable agreement, understand that some clauses in this agreement may not be legally enforceable. Nonetheless, it is agreed that while the parties enter into this agreement as a whole, they also agree to enter into each separate provision of this agreement as if it were a separate agreement.

2. Each party to this agreement hereby confirms that the foregoing has been entered into without any undue influence or fraud or coercion or misrepresentation whatsoever and that each has read the herein agreement in its entirety and with full knowledge of the contents hereof and does hereinafter affix his or her signature voluntarily hereto.

3. The parties further covenant and agree to do and execute all further assurances and other instruments that may be required or necessary by either of them to give full effect to the terms contained in this agreement.

4. The words "the future Wife" and "the future Husband" are used in this agreement only to identify the parties. Except as otherwise expressly provided herein, no right or obligation herein created or reserved or imposed, shall cease to be impaired or affected in any way if the parties marry or the marriage between the parties is dissolved or annulled.

5. If the marriage does not take place, this agreement shall be in all respects and for all purposes null and void.

6. Each party hereby acknowledges that all matters embodied herein as well as all questions pertinent hereto have been fully and satisfactorily explained to them; that they have given due consideration to such matters and questions; that they clearly understand and consent to all the provisions herein; that they have been fully advised by their respective solicitors of their rights and liabilities; and that they are each entering into this agreement freely, voluntarily, and with full knowledge.

7. This agreement shall enure to the benefit of and shall be binding on the heirs, executors, and administrators of the parties.

8. The validity and interpretation of this agreement and of each clause and part thereof shall be governed by the law of the Province of British Columbia.

IN WITNESS WHEREOF the parties hereto have hereunto set their hands and seals.

SIGNED, SEALED AND
DELIVERED
in the presence of:

Walter Witness   _Betty Bliss_

Walter Witness
1234 West 5th Avenue
Burnaby, British Columbia
Salesman
As to the signature of Betty Bliss

in the presence of:

Wilma Witness   _Larry Lonely_

Wilma Witness
1234 West 5th Avenue
Burnaby, British Columbia
Homemaker
As to the signature of Larry Lonely

MARRIAGE CONTRACT

THIS AGREEMENT made in quadruplicate this 15th day of June, 19-.

BETWEEN:

> MARY MATRI, in the City of Vancouver,
> in the Province of British Columbia
> (hereinafter called "the Wife")

> OF THE FIRST PART

—AND—

> MARTIN MATRI, of the City of Vancouver,
> in the Province of British Columbia
> (hereinafter called "the Husband")

> OF THE SECOND PART

WITNESSES to the fact that the Husband and Wife (as the parties in this contract should be called) were married each to the other on the 10th day of May, 19-;

AND to the fact that the Husband and Wife have considered the present and future conduct and course of their marriage and have reached certain conclusions as to their relationship which they wish to have reduced to writing;

AND to the fact that the Husband and Wife wish to enter into a formal binding agreement with respect to the future marriage relationship and to be bound in law in that regard insofar as it is possible, and where the provisions of their agreement are not binding in law, to express their intention one to the other with respect to the matrimonial relationship they are attempting to develop and establish;

AND to the fact that although the marriage contract in its very nature is a contract for life, and is accepted as such by the parties hereto, that there do arise situations beyond the control of the parties hereto that make it inevitable that there be a separation of the parties and that the Husband and Wife wish to provide for that eventuality;

AND to the fact that each has disclosed to the other all of his or her estate, property, and prospects for now and the future and that each is fully conversant with the estate, property, and prospects of the other;

AND WHEREAS at the time of marriage, friends and relatives of both the Husband and the Wife gave marriage presents to each respectively which now constitute their separate property;

AND WHEREAS the Husband has been employed since the marriage and presently is employed as a plumber and receives $16 000 a year in wages;

AND WHEREAS the Wife has been employed for remuneration since the celebration of the marriage and has savings accumulated from that time in her own savings account and is now in receipt of a monthly family allowance cheque;

AND WHEREAS the parties intend this agreement to be a marriage agreement within the meaning of the Family Relations Act, 1978;

NOW THEREFORE IN CONSIDERATION of the mutual promises in this agreement, and in consideration of the mutual love and affection each bears to the other, the Husband and Wife agree as follows:

(From this point the same clauses used in the pre-marriage contract, starting with Article I, may be adapted for use in the marriage contract.)

3. Property agreements

Many people who have been married for some time wish to enter into a marriage contract solely to settle the property relationship between themselves since the questions of children and work around the house have usually been settled already. (See Sample #3.)

In drawing up the contract, the important points to include are a statement to the effect that the parties wish the contract to be enforced by a court of law (since there is a presumption that the contracts made by married couples are not intended to be so enforceable) and a clause indicating that both parties do, in fact, have property to bestow on the other since mutual love and affection are not valuable considerations in the eyes of the law.

You should follow up the agreement by signing the necessary documents for filing in the Land Title Office putting the property into both spouses' names. A third person, such as a mortgage company or a purchaser, would not be bound by a property agreement such as the above. Third parties are entitled to rely on the title to the property as it appears in the Land Title Office.

e. COMMON-LAW MARRIAGES — WRITTEN CONTRACTS

As mentioned earlier, couples who live in a common-law relationship acquire limited rights and obligations under the Family Relations Act. For example, as mentioned earlier, the Family Relations Act embodies the concept that a husband and wife, upon separation or divorce, will share equally in any property ordinarily used for a family purpose. There is no equivalent law for parties who have never married. For this reason, a contract may be more important in such relationships. If you are agreed that you hold a joint interest in certain assets, obviously the best protection in cases of real property (land) is to have both names on the title. The same is true for such items as cars, boats, trailers, and other items requiring registration. Failing that, it would seem important to have a written contract setting out the intentions. Otherwise the "wife" may find she has contributed untold hours of labor on a farm, for example, owned by her "husband" and not have a leg to stand on in court when the break-up comes and she is claiming her share.

SAMPLE #3
PROPERTY AGREEMENT

THIS DEED OF AGREEMENT made in quadruplicate the 20th day of August, 19-.

BETWEEN:

HARRIET HOMEY, homemaker, of Vancouver, in the Province of British Columbia (hereinafter called "the Wife")

OF THE FIRST PART

—AND—

HARRY HOMEY, bus driver, of Vancouver, in the Province of British Columbia (hereinafter called "the Husband")

OF THE SECOND PART

WHEREAS the parties to this agreement are husband and wife and wish to set out the terms under which all property now owned by them and which will be acquired by them during the course of the marriage will be held and which at a later time may be enforced by a court of law;

AND WHEREAS the Wife is presently the owner of a 1983 Pontiac motor vehicle, a savings account of $100, furniture, and miscellaneous property (which was paid for by the Wife from her independent income) and is in receipt of an independent income in the form of a family allowance;

AND WHEREAS the Husband is the owner of an acreage located near Whistler in the Province of British Columbia a 1986 Ford motor vehicle, a savings account of $150, furniture, and miscellaneous property, and is presently in receipt of an independent income from the B.C. Transit System.

NOW THEREFORE THIS AGREEMENT WITNESSETH that in consideration of the mutual covenants herein contained, IT IS AGREED as follows:

1. The Wife hereby gives a half interest in all real or personal property owned by her or that will be acquired by her during the course of her cohabitation with the Husband with the exception of items and gifts used only by the Wife which shall include, without limiting the generality of the foregoing, to camera equipment and sewing machine.

2. The Husband hereby gives a half interest in all real or personal property owned by him or that will be acquired by him during the course of his cohabitation with the Wife with the exception of items and gifts used only by the Husband that shall include, without limiting the generality of the foregoing, tools.

3. This contract may be dissolved by either party upon one month's notice in writing to the other. After one month has elapsed,

either party may demand of the other an accounting and any transfers of legal title of property necessary in order that a division of the assets of the party may be made in accordance with the terms of this contract.

IN WITNESS WHEREOF we have hereunto set out hands and seals as of the day and year before mentioned.

SIGNED, SEALED and DELIVERED
in the presence of:

I.M. Witness

I.M. Witness
1234 West 5th Street
Burnaby, British Columbia
Salesman
As to the signature of Harriet Homey

Harriet Homey

I.C. Ewe

I.C. Ewe
1234 West 5th Street
Burnaby, British Columbia
Accountant
As to the signature of Harry Homey

Harry Homey

2
SEPARATION AND SEPARATION AGREEMENTS

a. WHEN THE HONEYMOON IS OVER, WHERE DO I TURN FOR HELP?

When a marriage or other relationship between two people begins to disintegrate, you may wish to seek assistance by obtaining legal advice and/or some type of counselling.

1. Legal counselling

Legal counselling is important for protection because of the changing and sometimes ambiguous situation that may exist. Unfortunately, consulting a lawyer tends to be considered an aggressive rather than conciliatory step and may have a negative influence on your chances of getting together again.

If you wish legal advice but still intend to make a serious attempt at reconciliation, you should either fully disclose to your partner your intent to seek legal advice and seek the partner's approval, or the legal advice should be sought in complete secrecy. Legal advice should never be used as a lever as then it will only aggravate whatever relationship still exists.

When you consult a lawyer for purposes of merely seeking advice, not wanting to further disrupt an already troubled marriage relationship, make very clear to the lawyer that you still wish to keep open all possible channels for reconciliation. The lawyer should be very carefully instructed to take no steps that could be damaging to this end and, possibly, to do nothing until you have had further opportunity to explore the situation.

2. Other counselling

Even if legal advice is sought, however, it is frequently wise to obtain some type of counselling. This can be related to two specific goals: either reconciliation (getting back together again) or conciliation (trying to sort out the problems with a minimum amount of difficulty and dispute).

Counselling may well serve to save a disintegrating relationship. It is sometimes surprising what a difference the independent views of a third party can make in such a situation. Even if you and your spouse have passed the point of *wanting* to save the relationship, counselling may well assist you to end your unhappy marriage with less social, psychological, and economic costs. There are a growing number of professionals entering the arena of mediation including doctors, lawyers, social workers, and psychologists.

3. Financial problems

Financial problems can be of considerable difficulty for a family and put tremendous pressure on the marriage relationship. In such a situation, a local banker might be able to offer useful advice or, if not, recommend someone who could. There is also another book in the Self-Counsel Legal Series entitled *Credit, Debt, and Bankruptcy*, which is a useful source of information and advice.

4. Mental health problems

If there is a problem involving mental disorder or breakdown, doctors and psychiatrists are available on a professional basis. If money is a problem, there are, of course, the public medical health insurance programs and public health facilities to which you may go for assistance. Again, access to these facilities can be obtained through family court or the offices of the Ministry of Social Services and Housing.

These services are sometimes difficult to locate and per-severance may be necessary to establish contact. In many cases, the wife is willing to see a counsellor but the husband is reluctant. Sometimes this is merely embarrassment but an absolute refusal to take these steps is a clear signal that the marriage is on the verge of a breakdown. Also, if the people in the marriage relationship have gone beyond the point of caring or have withdrawn into a total self-first attitude, it is likely too late for any amount of counselling to be of assis-tance. At this point, the other partner should refer quickly to the later chapters of this book for advice.

If, despite the advice and counselling referred to above, the matrimonial problems continue, the parties may have to face the prospect of separating and living apart. What then?

b. WHAT IS A LEGAL SEPARATION?

You walk into your lawyer's office and say you want "a legal separation." There is no such thing; the term is meaningless in British Columbia law. A husband and wife are legally separated when they live separate and apart from each other.

However, when a husband and wife separate, there are certain rights that each may assert and corresponding obliga-tions that each may be called upon to fulfill. The assertion and enforcement of these rights and obligations can be done either through mutual agreement or by adjudication in the courts.

These rights and obligations may involve not only the spouses, but also the children of the marriage. The most fre-quent issues arising between husband and wife can be categorized as follows: custody, access, and maintenance of children; maintenance and support; title and possession of property; and divorce. Each of these categories is more thoroughly dealt with in succeeding chapters of this book. A court may deal with each type of problem separately or com-bine some of them in one court action. It is not necessary for a spouse to apply for a divorce before asserting one of these claims.

If neither spouse wishes to make a "claim" against the other, they merely have to establish separate residences and become "legally" separated. This type of "clean-break" happens infrequently. In the majority of cases there are at least some rights and obligations that must be either agreed upon or settled by the courts.

c. SEPARATION AGREEMENTS EXPLAINED

At one time it was the law that one spouse could take action in the courts to force the other spouse to live with him or her. This, in effect, was an enforcement of one of the unwritten terms of the marriage contract. However, such an action has been abolished.

The law as it now stands is that two people, whether they are married or not, who have lived together by consent for any length of time can separate at any time merely by one or the other deciding to move out. It is that simple and there is no legal requirement that the parties move back together. The separation is legal. There may be strings that one person has on the other such as children, property, or money, and which person moves out first may have considerable legal implication, but that does not affect the fact that the separation itself is legal.

Having said that, we must add that the court certainly looks beyond the question of *who* moved out to find out *why* he or she moved out. Many lay people are afraid to make the break, even though it's certainly justified by their circumstances, because of the fear that they will automatically be viewed by the court as the "bad guy." Not so.

The exact nature of the relationship that one party has with the other after the separation depends on the individual circumstances of the separation and on the legal status of the parties with respect to each other and their conduct leading up to the separation. All of these matters are discussed later.

When parties do separate, or are in the process of planning their separation, they can enter into a contract, which is really just a written agreement setting out the terms and conditions under which they are separating; such things as who gets the car, the kids, the house, and the debt payments are sorted out on paper. This document is frequently called a legal separation. However, as we have pointed out, all separations are legal and lawyers usually refer to such documents as separation agreements. They are usually drawn by a lawyer but there is no necessity for this whatsoever and any document drawn by the parties and signed by themselves will have value.

As stated before, the courts are much more inclined to enforce such an agreement if the parties have had separate legal counsel. Thus, ideally, the separation agreement should be drawn by a lawyer and one party should sign in front of that lawyer, the other party in front of a separate lawyer so that each gets independent advice as to the true legal effect of the action. Regardless of whatever old wives' tales and rumors exist about the effectiveness of separation agreements, they are legally very powerful and should not be entered into lightly. An example of a typical separation agreement is shown in Sample #4.

No one can be forced to sign a separation agreement and, should that happen, a court will rapidly overturn the agreement and reconsider the whole situation. As has already been mentioned, an agreement that both parties can live with is frequently preferable to an enforced settlement on the basis of legal rights and duties.

As with a marriage agreement, a separation agreement can provide for the ownership and division of property, support obligations, the right to direct the education and moral training of the children, and any other matter required in the settlement of affairs. The contract can specifically provide for the custody of, and access to, children and, generally, the court will enforce this provision unless it is totally contrary to the best interests and welfare of the children. The contract can also provide for who is to have the right to live in the matrimonial home.

Should you ever be in a position of wanting to change the terms of a separation agreement, you will require the advice of a lawyer. One final point here: getting an agreement changed is difficult, so, before signing, make sure it says what you want it to say and covers all the relevant points.

1. What value is a separation agreement and can it be enforced?

It is often heard that separation agreements are of no value. Equally, one frequently hears that the law is of no value. This is because the law — and separation agreements — are like hammers. A hammer on a work bench will not get up and drive nails for you. You have to pick it up and use it. The law is the same; it is a tool to be used, and if the separation agreement is being broken by your spouse, the law will not jump in and enforce it for you. You must take up the law and use it to enforce your rights.

The advantages of having a separation agreement are numerous. First, the existence of a separation agreement is an incentive to avoid litigation. It is always preferable to settle your disputes as quickly and as painlessly as possible. If you get involved in litigation, the results may be unpredictable, the procedure lengthy, the emotional trauma considerable, and the expense substantial.

Second, if you are making payments for the support of your spouse or children, you may deduct these payments from your gross income to compute your taxable income, provided that you fulfill the following conditions:

(a) The payments must be made to your spouse directly, or to a third party with the consent and for the benefit of your spouse (e.g., to the mortgage company if the spouse lives in the matrimonial home).

(b) The payments must be for the benefit of the spouse or children or both.

(c) The payments must be periodic; a lump sum, even though it may be payable in instalments, is not deductible.

(d) The payments must be made pursuant to a written separation agreement or an order of the court.

For tax purposes, your spouse will have to include in his or her income all payments that you properly deduct. If the payments do not meet all of the above conditions, however, they are not deductible and, therefore, your spouse need pay no tax on them. The following examples illustrate the tax consequences.

EXAMPLE A:

Mr. and Mrs. Breakdown entered into a separation agreement in 198- whereby Mr. Breakdown pays Mrs. Breakdown the following sums:

(a) $300 per month to Mrs. Breakdown for her own maintenance

(b) $150 per month to Mrs. Breakdown for each of their two children — Jonathan, 17 years old and Joanne, 10 years old

(c) $150 per month to the Honorable Trust Company, the mortgagee on the former matrimonial home occupied by Mrs. Breakdown and the children

(d) $1 500 to Dr. Cuspid, for orthodontic work for Joanne

Mr. Breakdown earns a salary of $20 000 per year. Mrs. Breakdown has no other sources of income.

Mr. Breakdown's tax may be computed as follows:

Gross income		$20 000
Deductions:		
Personal	$4 220	
Support payments (a), (b) and (c)	9 000	
Total	$13 220	
Taxable income		$ 6 780

Note: Mr. Breakdown is unable to claim the $1 500 medical expenses because he has not claimed the children as dependants on his tax return.

Mrs. Breakdown's tax may be computed as follows:

Gross income		$9 000
Deductions:		
Personal	$4 220	
First child (married equivalent)	3 700	
Second child (under 18 years)*	560	
Total	$8 480	
Taxable income		$520

*The deduction for a child 18 or older is $1 200.

EXAMPLE B:

The facts are the same as example A except that Mr. Breakdown does not pay maintenance to Mrs. Breakdown directly, and Mrs. Breakdown earns $8 000 per year as a secretary.

Mr. Breakdown's tax can be computed as follows:

Gross income		$20 000
Deductions:		
Personal	$4 220	
Support payments	5 400	
Total	$9 620	
Taxable income		$10 380

Mrs. Breakdown's tax can be computed as follows:

Gross income from employment		$ 8 000
Gross income from support payments		5 400
Total		$13 400
Deductions:		
Personal	$4 220	
First child	3 700	
Second child	560	
Total	$8 480	
Taxable income		$4 920

A third advantage of separation agreements that must be considered is that courts are bound by certain rules and there are only certain kinds of orders they can make. On the other hand, parties entering into a separation agreement are free to contract for almost any form of settlement that they think fit. In other words, they can enter into types of arrangements that the courts would not want to order and so a separation agreement has greater flexibility and potential convenience for the parties concerned.

Fourth, separation agreements do not stand in the way of further court action regarding divorce, maintenance, or custody of children, especially when the circumstances radically change from the date of the signing of the agreement. Also, they do not stand in the way of reconciliation of the parties and most agreements contain clauses that allow for reconciliation attempts. In cases in which all the parties are in agreement or in which there is no valid reason for having them changed, the provisions of the separation agreement can be adopted by the judge and made into a formal court order in a divorce action or proceedings in family court.

Lastly, the date a separation agreement is signed is important when there is matrimonial property to be appraised and divided. British Columbia does not have true community property laws in which both spouses share equally in family assets *throughout* their relationship. Rather, there is "deferred community property." Simply put, this means a husband or wife is entitled to a one-half interest in each family asset after the relationship ends (i.e., when a separation agreement is signed or a divorce is granted). the date is important because of the fluctuation in value of family assets, especially real estate. For example, if a couple sign a separation agreement in November, 1987, but don't actually divide their assets until November, 1989, the court would look at how much the matrimonial home and other family assets were worth on November 1987, not November, 1989. (Remember, this law affecting matrimonial property pertains to legal marriages only, not common-law relationships.)

2. Topics in a separation agreement

Although there is generally no limit to the issues that can be covered in a separation agreement, the most common matters dealt with include the following:

(a) Maintenance and support between husband and wife (see chapter 4)

(b) Custody, access, and maintenance of children (see chapter 5)

(c) Release of any interest one party may have against the estate of the other in the event of death

(d) Maintenance and payment of premiums of life insurance policy by husband naming wife or children as beneficiaries

(e) Division of matrimonial assets that may include stocks, bonds, personal chattels and real property such as house, cottage, or vacant land (see chapter 6)

(f) Release from further claims and agreement not to claim for further maintenance or support by way of litigation

3. What happens if one spouse fails to live up to the agreement?

Like any other agreement, if one party seeks to break it, there is going to be a hassle. But if this happens, the agreement has great strength. The maintenance provisions, if any, are a debt, enforceable in court like any other debt. They also carry great weight when it comes to seeking maintenance orders in family court or Supreme Court. Provisions regarding children and property made by the parties will generally be enforced by the courts if they are not contrary to public policy and are in the best interests of the children.

To simplify enforcement, it is advisable to register your separation agreement with the provincial court, family division. This requires sending a copy of the signed agreement to the court closest to your home together with consent forms as set out in Sample #5 signed by each of the parties to the agreement. As you see, it is necessary to sign the consent form before a lawyer or notary public.

The advantage of registering the separation agreement is that it makes the provisions about maintenance, custody, and access enforceable by the court just as though you actually had a court order covering those items. To illustrate the difference, suppose you have a separation agreement that required your spouse to pay child support of $200 per month. Six months have gone by in which no payments have been made. If the agreement has not been registered, you would have to start an action for maintenance or, alternatively, sue your spouse on the basis of the separation agreement — just as though it was a contract between two unrelated parties. If you followed that course of action, you would find yourself, after going through all the legal procedure, in receipt of an order — or judgment — against your spouse in the amount of $1 200 (the amount of the arrears). Then you would have to worry about how to enforce your order by garnishee proceedings. If the agreement is registered with family court, it is as though you already have that order and you can get right on with enforcing it (see chapter 4).

The legal value of the agreement aside, if you have taken the time to sit down and discuss how you want the separation to be conducted and what terms and provisions you want included in it, you are more likely to carry on with and abide by your agreement. The very act of entering into the agreement has value. And, upon any subsequent court hearing, the agreement is extremely good evidence as to what the parties originally intended.

The courts do not view with sympathy people who change their minds, and the person seeking to overturn a binding agreement that he or she signed must have a very strong and good reason for going so. If it was good enough for you to have signed originally, then the obvious question is "Why has it now ceased to become so?".

Where one party is in breach of any of the terms of the separation agreement, the other party may treat the agreement as being cancelled. For example, if the husband promises to pay a certain sum of money for the maintenance of the wife on a weekly basis and neglects or fails to make such payments, the wife may institute proceedings for maintenance. She will not be bound by the amount stated in the agreement, despite the fact that she had agreed not to make a claim for further support. In other words, she may ask the court to disregard the agreement because her husband disregarded it.

As mentioned, if she is content with the amount provided for in the agreement, she may sue her husband for the arrears. With the exception of the provisions dealing with the children, the court will not give any consideration to the appropriateness of the agreement and will merely require the husband to pay the arrears. A husband has few defences available in this type of court proceeding.

If one party attempts to break a separation agreement, the other party should immediately seek the advise of a lawyer for, as you can see, the matters to be considered are numerous and sometimes complex.

4. How effective is a separation agreement when I get a divorce?

You may think it strange, but the divorce court actually has the power to disregard a written separation agreement. This is because the Divorce Act gives the court supreme jurisdiction in determining the questions of custody, access, child support, and interspousal support. However, if the separation agreement has been entered into fairly, both parties have had independent legal advice, and the circumstances of the parties have not changed by the time the divorce is heard, the court will give it considerable, if not conclusive, weight in deciding the issues. Otherwise, the court may merely adjudicate the issues on the basis of the evidence presented at the trial.

SAMPLE #4
SEPARATION AGREEMENT

THIS AGREEMENT made in triplicate this 27th day of June, A.D. 19-

BETWEEN:

> JACK JAMES SPLITUPP, Carpenter, of 5555
> 55th Street, Wilton, British Columbia
> (hereinafter called "the Husband")
>
> > OF THE FIRST PART

—AND—

> JUDY JILL SPLITUPP, Housewife, of 1293
> 68th Avenue, Wilton, British Columbia
> (hereinafter called "the Wife")
>
> > OF THE SECOND PART

WHEREAS the parties hereto are Husband and Wife and were married on the 4th day of August, A.D. 1971 at Vancouver, British Columbia;

AND WHEREAS the parties hereto have two children, namely:

JILL SPLITUPP, born in Wilton, British Columbia, June 24, 1979

ROBERT SPLITUPP, born in Wilton, British Columbia, December 20, 1985;

AND WHEREAS the Husband and the Wife have agreed to live separate and apart and did commence to live separate and apart, on or about the 1st day of September, A.D. 1988 upon terms and conditions hereinafter expressed;

AND WHEREAS each party is fully advised and fully informed of the estate and prospects of the other party and the parties have been severally advised and informed by their respective solicitors of their respective rights and liabilities against and to each other and to and with reference to the property and estate of each other;

AND WHEREAS the parties desire to provide for the orderly settlement of their affairs and their respective rights and obligations upon separation and subsequently upon dissolution of the marriage or upon death as particularly set out herein;

NOW THEREFORE THIS AGREEMENT WITNESSES that in consideration of the premises and in consideration of the mutual covenants, agreements and undertakings herein set out, the parties hereby expressly agree as follows:

1. THE PROPER LAW of this contract shall be the law of the Province of British Columbia, and this contract shall also be deemed to be valid and enforceable in accordance with the law of any other jurisdiction. The parties intend all of their affairs and property to be governed by this contract and the law of British Columbia, and, without restricting the generality of the foregoing, jointly and severally declare that the contract provides each spouse with the interest in each family asset to which he or she is entitled upon marriage breakup, as provided for in the Family Relations Act RSBC 1979, c. 121, s. 43 et. seq.

2. THE PARTIES will, during the currency of this agreement, live separate and apart from each other as though each were unmarried and each will henceforth be free from the control and authority of the other, and shall reside and may reside at such place or places and in such manner as he or she shall see fit, and may work at any employment or carry on any business as he or she may see fit or proper, and shall not at any time hereafter require the other to live with him or her, nor shall either party institute any legal proceedings against the other for restitution or conjugal rights or molest or annoy or interfere with the other in any manner whatsoever.

3. IF AT anytime during the currency of this agreement the Husband and Wife shall by mutual consent agree to cohabit as Husband and Wife then and in such case this agreement shall become null and void and of no further effect; PROVIDED THAT, resumption of cohabitation during any period of not more than ninety (90) days, when such cohabitation is resumed or continued with reconciliation

as the primary purpose, shall not compromise this agreement nor shall it compromise the running of time toward the time when, under the Divorce Act, a divorce becomes possible on the grounds that the spouses have been living separate and apart for not less than one year.

4. THE HUSBAND agrees that the Wife shall have, forthwith after execution hereof, full custody of the infant children of the marriage, namely, JILL SPLITUPP and ROBERT SPLITUPP, above described; PROVIDED THAT the Husband shall have generous access to the said children, such rights of visitation to include overnight, weekends and vacations by prior arrangement with the Wife; PROVIDED FURTHER that the children shall, by prior arrangement and with the consent of each child spend Easter, Christmas and summer vacations with either of the parties and neither of the parties shall unreasonably withhold consent to such vacation visits; AND FURTHER PROVIDED that such visiting and vacation provisions may be varied from time to time as the children reach certain ages where they, or either of them, can reasonably be removed from the care and control of the Wife for periods of time consistent with the state of their or his development, health and general well-being, consent to which proposed variations shall not be unreasonably withheld by the Wife.

5. EACH OF THE PARTIES hereto agree that if the Wife either dies or becomes physically incapacitated and unable to care for the children of the marriage, then custody of the children of the marriage shall revert to the Husband; PROVIDED THAT such custody is acceptable to the child or children affected.

6. THE WIFE and Husband agree that they shall have joint responsibility for making decisions with respect to the education, including choice of schools; health care, including choice of doctors, dentists, and surgeons; summer plans, such as the choice of camps and trips; and the general welfare of the children, and reserve the right to be consulted with respect to each or all of the foregoing, and further, reserve the right to have those matters, or any one of them, referred to a mediator pursuant to the provisions of paragraph 40 of this agreement.

7. THE HUSBAND and Wife each agree that the children may be removed from the place where they are to reside, for a visit with the Husband, but if the children are to be removed from the Province of British Columbia, they, or either of them, may only be removed by prior agreement of the Wife and upon the undertaking of the Husband to return them, or either of them, to the possession of the Wife at the residence of the Wife, as it may be from time to time.

8. THE WIFE agrees to continue to reside with the children in the City of Wilton, Province of British Columbia, for the purpose of giving full effect to the access provisions of clause 4 above; PROVIDED THAT if it becomes necessary for the Wife to move out of the City of Wilton to other places within the Province of British Columbia for the purpose of seeking or maintaining suitable employment the Husband will not unreasonably refuse to agree to such relocation as may be necessary from time to time.

9. THE HUSBAND and Wife agree that in the event of serious illness of the children, or either of them, each will give the other prompt notice of such illness, but that the party in whose custody the child is at the time of such occurrence may, without reference to the other, arrange for emergency care.

10. THE HUSBAND and Wife covenant and agree, from the time of commencement of this agreement, to be jointly responsible for the payment of all and whatever is necessary for the support and education of the children of the marriage, regardless of where they may be resident from time to time, and neither remarriage nor commencement of cohabitation by either or both of them with a third person will relieve them of this responsibility; PROVIDED THAT such payments for the children, or either of them, are to continue until the respective child reaches the age of nineteen (19) years, unless he or she sooner marries or leaves school, in either of which events the support payable by the Husband and Wife shall, at the option of either the Husband or the Wife, cease; AND PROVIDED ALSO that if the children, or either of them, continue his or her education beyond the age of nineteen (19) years, such payments for support shall continue in respect of the children, or child, until the education to the first post-secondary school certificate or degree is completed in a timely manner.

11. THE HUSBAND covenants and agrees that he will provide to the Wife the sum of One Hundred and Fifty Dollars ($150.00) per month per child for their maintenance and support making together the sum of Three Hundred Dollars ($300.00) per month for the two children during the time and under the conditions set forth in clause 10 above.

12. THE HUSBAND covenants and agrees that he will pay to the Wife for her maintenance and support during the period of time in which she is completing her education at the University of British Columbia the sum of Four Hundred and Fifty Dollars ($450.00) per month and thereafter will continue to pay the sum of Four Hundred and Fifty Dollars ($450.00) per month until she finds employment or for a period of three (3) years or until divorce whichever is the soonest.

13. THE HUSBAND covenants and agrees that he will, for the purpose of giving full effect to paragraphs 6 and 10, above, make additional payments with respect to the maintenance and support of the children of the marriage, which from time to time may be appropriate as a result of: emergency; medical, dental and surgical expenses, hospitalization and the like; and, with respect to the tuition of the children, or either child of the marriage, who may be a worthy candidate for college or university education.

14. THE HUSBAND covenants and agrees to maintain health insurance coverage including medical, hospital, surgical coverage and to pay for such items as eye glasses and prosthetic devices as and when required, only on behalf of the children of the marriage, in specific fulfilment of his responsibilities for performance of these provisions of the Agreement, and to maintain such coverage with respect to the Wife until she becomes employed or until she is no longer qualified, for whatever reason, to be included under the insurance plans available to him through his employer.

15. THE HUSBAND covenants and agrees to pay the cost of all necessary dental care for the children of the marriage PROVIDED THAT a Dental Insurance Plan being available at the Husband's place of employment. THE HUSBAND COVENANTS AND AGREES to take and maintain dental insurance coverage with respect to the

children of the marriage in specific fulfilment of his responsibilities for performance of this provision of the Agreement, and to maintain such coverage with respect to the Wife until she becomes employed or until she is no longer qualified, for whatever reason, to be included under the insurance plans available to him through his employer.

16. THE HUSBAND AGREES that he will support the children to the extent set out above as well after as before divorce and that the support terms of the agreement are to be binding upon his executors, heirs and assigns.

17. THE HUSBAND AGREES to permit the Wife and children to have possession and occupancy of the matrimonial home at 1293 68 Avenue, in the City of Wilton, Province of British Columbia, more particularly known and described as,

> City of Wilton
> Lot 52
> Block 28
> District Lot 2027
> Plan 1584

without requiring the payment of occupational rent, for the same period of time during which she receives the sum of Four Hundred and Fifty Dollars ($450.00) per month for her own maintenance and support as set out in clause 12 above.

18. THE HUSBAND AND THE WIFE covenant and agree that the Wife holds title to the matrimonial home in her name alone upon a resulting trust with respect to one-half undivided moitey for the Husband; AND THE WIFE AGREES that when she is no longer entitled, pursuant to the provisions of clauses 12 and 17 above, to occupy the matrimonial home without payment of occupational rent that she will do all things necessary, in concert with the Husband, to expeditiously sell the house; AND THE HUSBAND AND WIFE AGREE that the net proceeds from the sale of the matrimonial home at the above-noted future time will be equally divided between them.

19. EACH OF THE PARTIES AGREES, that in the event of the death of either of the parties the interest of that party in the fee simple with respect to the matrimonial home, whether vested or in expectancy, will pass to the surviving party as though the parties were registered as joint tenants, and as though this Agreement did not exist, for so long as this Agreement is executory; AND EACH FURTHER AGREES that when the time set out in paragraphs 12 and 17 above has run, the fee simple in the matrimonial home shall vest in them as tenants in common and until the matrimonial home is sold and the net proceeds have been distributed each shall be free to dispose of his interest by sale, or, upon death, by testamentary disposition or, in the event of intestacy, as provided in the Estate Administration Act, 1979 RSBC c. 114.

20. THE WIFE covenants and agrees to make all of the monthly payments on the mortgage on the matrimonial home including principal, interest and taxes; AND THE WIFE FURTHER agrees to indemnify and save harmless the Husband from any liability however arising from the mortgage on the matrimonial home presently standing in her name as the mortgagor, and without limiting the generality of the foregoing to save him harmless from any claim whatsoever against him as guarantor of the first mortgage against the matrimonial home.

21. THE WIFE covenants and agrees to pay for all current and routine maintenance required, from time to time, to keep the matrimonial home in proper trim and repair and to pay all costs incurred for those purposes.

22. EACH OF THE PARTIES agrees that in the event any improvements or alterations are to be made to the house that neither party will have the right or privilege of committing the other to the payment of any costs incurred but both parties agree that the costs of such alterations and improvements may be negotiated between the parties PROVIDED THAT neither party shall be under any obligation to consent to payment of all or part of the cost of any such alterations or improvements.

23. EACH OF THE PARTIES agrees that the matrimonial home may be sold and the net proceeds divided equally upon any one of the following occurring:

(a) If at any time both Husband and Wife agree to the sale of the matrimonial home, notwithstanding any other provision in this agreement;

(b) If the Wife, for any reason, voluntarily vacates the matrimonial home for a continuous period of more than thirty days; or,

(c) If the Wife permits the mortgage to fall into arrears and does not bring it into good standing within thirty days of the default, upon the occurrence of any of which events the Husband will be excused from further performance of his promises under Paragraph 17, above, and the WIFE AGREES that the Husband may, at his sole option register the quit claim deed with respect to a one-half interest in the matrimonial home, which the Wife will provide to him upon execution of this agreement.

24. THE WIFE AND THE HUSBAND covenant and agree to cooperate each with the other in offering the matrimonial home for sale when it becomes available for sale under the terms of this agreement; and each of the parties further agree to execute all documents necessary for the listing and sale of the matrimonial home pursuant to this and other clauses in the agreement at their own separate costs and expense and to instruct their respective solicitors to enter into appropriate undertakings between solicitors to ensure the full protection of the respective interests of the husband and of the wife under this agreement.

25. THE HUSBAND covenants and agrees to make all payments and assume all obligations of the marriage incurred up to and including the date of separation and, without limiting the generality of the foregoing to pay all bills including up to the date these presents including any charges incurred by way of credit card by either Husband or Wife, and the Husband agrees that he will keep the Wife indemnified therefrom and save harmless the Wife from and against

all liabilities hereinafter contracted or encountered by the Husband and all claims, actions, and demands on account thereof and all costs, charges, damages, and expenses to which the Wife may be put by reason of, or on account thereof.

26. THE WIFE covenants, at all future times, to keep the Husband indemnified against all debts and liabilities hereinafter contracted or incurred by the Wife, against any and all action or actions, proceedings, claims, demands, costs, damages and expenses whatsoever in respect thereof, and will not pledge the credit of the Husband, and if the Wife incurs any additional debts, whether for NECESSARIES or otherwise, while the Husband is not in default under the maintenance and support clauses of this contract, the Husband is to have the right to reduce the payments to the Wife by the amount he has to pay with respect to those debts.

27. THE WIFE shall not continue to be a beneficiary of any existing policy of life insurance on the life of the Husband, which insurance the Husband binds himself to maintain in force for the benefit of the children of the marriage and with respect to which he assigns all his right to the said children, AND the Wife covenants and agrees that she will do all things necessary to delete her name as beneficiary from the policy currently in effect on the life of the Husband, and shall and does, save as herein stated, hereby release to the Husband all and any interest she has, or may otherwise have obtained, in the existing or any future policy of insurance on the life of the Husband.

28. THE HUSBAND hereby releases to the Wife all and any interest he may otherwise have obtained in the existing or any future policy of insurance on the life of the Wife.

29. THE HUSBAND shall be absolutely entitled to:

(a) All his personal clothing, jewellery and effects wherever situate;

(b) 1987 Volkswagon, registered NJA 924;

(c) One-half interest in an Erickson 27-foot Watership I Boat subject to a mortgage against it in the amount of $14 000, with respect to which debt he shall be solely responsible;

(d) Stocks and bonds currently in his possession or standing in his name;

(e) All the power tools and equipment in and about the matrimonial premises and,

(f) One deep freeze unit and one vacuum cleaner, each of which is to be selected by the Wife.

30. THE HUSBAND acknowledges that he has received from the Wife all his chattels and effects and any chattels and effects in which he may have any right or claim, and without limiting the generality of the foregoing, including everything set out in the paragraph next above.

31. THE HUSBAND acknowledges that he is to pay all insurance premiums with respect to the house, the household contents, the boat, the automobile, and all other personalty in his possession, pursuant to this agreement.

32. THE WIFE shall be absolutely entitled to all her personal clothing, jewellery, and effects wherever situate, all furniture, furnishings, fixtures, equipment, silverware, and household effects in or about the matrimonial home or in storage as at the date of this agreement and the Husband hereby releases and quits claims to the Wife any right, title, or interest which he has or may have therein, except as otherwise provided in clause 29 of this agreement.

33. THE WIFE acknowledges that she has received from the Husband all her chattels and effects and any chattels and effects in which she may have any right or claim and, without limiting the generality of the foregoing, including everything set out in the paragraph next above.

34. THE HUSBAND AND WIFE agree that each has his or her own separate bank account and that the other is entitled to the contents of the bank account or accounts held in their names and each hereby relinquishes any claims he has or may have with respect to the account of the other, wherever those accounts may be situate.

35. THE PARTIES hereto for themselves, their heirs, executors, administrators, and assigns, that they will, from time to time and at

all times hereafter upon such reasonable request and at the costs of the other of them, his or her heirs, executors, administrators, or assigns, execute and do all further assurances and acts for the purpose of giving full effect to these presents contained.

36. EACH OF THE PARTIES hereto renounces and relinquishes all right, title, and interest in the estate of the other and all right to participate in, benefit from, or administer the estate of the other;

37. SUBJECT TO the provision of this agreement, the Wife hereby releases the Husband from any action that she now has or may have against the Husband for support, maintenance, interim alimony, permanent alimony, or otherwise for herself.

38. NOTHING in the agreement shall prevent either of the parties from taking or instituting proceedings for divorce as they may be advised according to law on the ground of conduct that may have occurred previous to the date of these presents.

39. EXCEPT as otherwise expressly provided herein, no right or obligation herein created, reserved, or imposed shall cease, or be impaired, or affected in any way if the parties are divorced; and THE TERMS of this agreement are to survive a subsequent divorce and are to be enforceable as though the parties hereto were still married.

40. If a dispute arises concerning this agreement, neither party shall commence court proceedings until the parties have attempted mediation. Dr. E.L. Smith shall act as mediator. If Dr. Smith is unable to act as mediator, the parties shall select an alternate mediator, and failing agreement, the wife shall select the mediator. The parties shall share equally the cost of mediation.

41. EACH OF THE PARTIES to this separation agreement covenants and agrees that the provisions of this agreement shall survive the occurrence of any and all events that have occurred or may in the future occur under Section 43 of the Family Relations Act, or upon death, insofar as the provisions relate to an orderly settlement of the distribution of property.

42. THE WORDS "Husband" and "Wife" are used in this agreement only to identify the parties.

43. WHEREVER the singular or masculine is used throughout this agreement, the same shall be construed as meaning the plural or the feminine where the context or the parties hereto so require.

44. AND IT IS EXPRESSLY AGREED between the parties hereto that all covenants, provisos, and agreement, rights, powers, privileges, exclusions, and liabilities contained in this agreement shall be read and held as made by and with and granted to and imposed upon the respective parties hereto and their respective heirs, executors, administrators, successors, and assigns, as if the words heirs, executors, administrators, successors, and assigns had been inscribed in all proper and necessary places.

IN WITNESS WHEREOF the parties hereto have executed this agreement as of the date first above written.

SIGNED, SEALED, AND DELIVERED BY JACK JAMES SPLITUPP in the presence of:

SIGNED, SEALED, AND DELIVERED BY JUDY JILL SPLITUPP in the presence of:

Jack James Splitupp

Judy Jill Splitupp

Larry Lawyer

Elsie Legal

SAMPLE #5
CONSENT FORM

I, JUDY JILL SPLITUPP, consent to the filing of the agreement annexed hereto in the Provincial Court of British Columbia and to the enforcement thereafter of all provisions as may be contained therein

(a) for custody of, maintenance for, or access to my child or children (if any); and

(b) for the payment of maintenance by one spouse to the other.

Sworn before me at City of
Wilton, in the Province of
British Columbia,

Judy Jill Splitup

this 2nd day of July, 198-.

J. M. Commissioner

A Commissioner for Taking
Affidavits for British Columbia

d. HOW DO I HANDLE DEPRESSION AND LONELINESS?

Immediately after the separation of a husband and wife (and possibly even during the process of the breakdown), one of the big problems faced by both parties is loneliness and depression. After years of having someone around, it is very hard to get used to the idea of living alone, and even more so when this is aggravated by the presence and responsibility of children as well as all the pressures and uncertainties of the break-up.

If you are not employed and have been left with the children, keep your days busy tending to them, getting your finances in order, and seeking the necessary guidance that you need. Again, this is the time to seek the assistance of a sensitive social worker, friends, family, your local minister, or any combination of these people. You should look for activities, even non-paying endeavors, to become involved in so that you do not have long hours with nothing to do.

Picking up the pieces of your life and carrying on will call for the greatest of will power and self-control. Keep in mind that you are one of many who have passed through these same problems and same feelings and you are experiencing nothing unusual. Plan your days one at a time and let the future take care of itself. Only time will settle that pain in the middle of your chest and that fear that makes your stomach ache. When you are finally through it and you have reached the other side, remember those who are still in the struggle and be kind to them whenever the opportunity arises.

e. WHAT IS DESERTION?

Desertion is a withdrawal from the matrimonial relationship without just cause or excuse and with the intention of terminating the marital cohabitation. But it is really an outmoded term now as far as the law is concerned. Under the old Divorce Act, a deserting spouse had to wait five years before he or she could be granted a divorce whereas if the spouses mutually agreed to separate, it meant only a three-year wait. As outlined in chapter 3, the new Divorce Act makes no reference to these terms. It just looks to see whether the spouses were living separate and apart for at least one year prior to starting the divorce proceedings. It doesn't matter who left whom.

The Family Relations Act does not consider desertion either. It sets out factors to be considered in making an award of spousal support or division of matrimonial property and conduct is *not* included.

f. HOW DO I GET MY SPOUSE OUT OF THE HOUSE?

Lawyers frequently encounter the problem of how one spouse, usually the wife, can remove the other from the family home. If the marriage has broken down irretrievably and separation is inevitable, the woman with children faces the difficult decision of whether or not she should move. Almost always the answer is that it would be far cheaper, simpler, and less upsetting to the children for the husband to move. However, in these situations the husband is usually not entirely rational.

Husband and wife almost always are considered to have an equal interest in the house and an equal right to live there. It can, therefore, be very difficult to get the husband out of the house without resorting to the courts. The test in British Columbia in determining whether an order ought to be made giving the wife exclusive possession of the home is that the wife must show that the shared use of the matrimonial home is a practical impossibility and that she be preferred as an occupant on a balance of convenience.

Before you can apply for an order giving you exclusive possession of the home, you must start an action for divorce or an action under the Family Relations Act for a declaration that you and your spouse have no reasonable prospect of reconciliation with each other. Your application for exclusive possession is then made to the Supreme Court. It is a "chambers motion," which means you don't appear and give evidence in person but rather the judge decides on the basis of sworn affidavits. This is a complex procedure and should not be attempted without the help of a lawyer.

Another more drastic way of achieving the same end, in a situation where there's been physical violence, is to charge your spouse with assault. If convicted, your spouse may be put on probation on the condition that he or she not enter the matrimonial premises. (See sections k. and l. following for more details.)

An alternative to the legal process is to simply put the husband's belongings outside the house and change the locks on the doors. However, there is no law against a man breaking into his own house, so this method may not work at all. The same comments apply to a wife and it is not uncommon for a husband to shut his wife out of the house. Whether or not her name is on the title, she too is entitled to break in. It is here that the problem of a difference in physical strength becomes crucial and the husband likely has the advantage.

If, as a wife, you find the situation intolerable and, for whatever reasons, cannot have your husband ejected, your best bet may be to temporarily relocate and bring a court action against your husband for sufficient support to enable you to live elsewhere. The various ways of doing this are discussed in chapter 4. Before taking such a drastic step however, you should consult with a lawyer.

Under the Family Relations Act, it's clear that the matrimonial home is a family asset and, as such, each party is almost certainly entitled to one-half of the value of the property *regardless of whose name the house is registered in.* If your spouse agrees to sell it, you merely list the house for sale in the ordinary way. If he or she doesn't agree, it is possible to apply to the court for an order for sale.

The court is almost certain to make such an order unless it means ousting the wife and children and leaving them in a financial position where it is impossible to obtain adequate alternative housing. In such situations, often the court postpones the sale until the children are older — perhaps until they have completed school.

Remember, these comments about joint ownership of the family home apply to *legal* marriages. In common-law situations, the house belongs to the person whose name is on the title unless and until the court says otherwise.

g. THE MECHANICS OF MOVING

Ideally, the spouses should discuss the move and the division of their belongings. If that is not possible, and you decide to leave without warning, don't clean out the house! Under the Family Relations Act, spouses are entitled to an equal division of furniture and household belongings upon separation or divorce, so take approximately one-half of the total value of the belongings. If have the children with you, make sure you have enough to accommodate their basic needs too. Taking far more than your share will only aggravate already difficult situation, and, in time, the court might order some of it returned to your spouse. This subject is discussed in more detail in chapter 6.

When considering the matter of financing the move, there are several sources of funds to think about. Credit cards in the name of the husband and wife can be used by the wife. If she is earning low wages or is on social assistance and owns no property, the creditors will look to the husband for payment.

The same applies to charge accounts at various stores that are in the husband's name or in joint names. If clothing and other necessaries for the children and the wife are required, they should be charged before the husband has an opportunity of cancelling the accounts. The word "necessaries" must be stressed as in any future dispute before the courts the judges will look to see whether or not the actions of the wife in her moving out were reasonable in the circumstances. Unfair advantage should not be taken of these charge accounts and credit cards, but they are certainly a source of funds and there is nothing improper about their reasonable and intelligent use by the wife.

Joint bank accounts in the name of both parties generally tend to belong equally to both in the eyes of the law. In some situations it may be considered advisable for the departing wife to remove funds from these accounts but again you should do what is reasonable in the circumstances. To merely clean out the bank account will be frowned upon in court.

If, following the move, you are in need of financial assistance, you can apply to the Ministry of Social Services and Housing for help. When you apply, you must sign a form giving up your right to claim support from your spouse. Instead, the government takes over that right and will bring an application in your name. If your spouse doesn't have enough income to wholly support you and/or the children, the ministry will make up the difference. You are allowed to keep $100 of the maintenance payment received each month without the amount of social assistance being reduced. Anything over that results in an equivalent reduction in the amount of social assistance. So, for example, if a husband is ordered to pay $200 per month for the support of his wife who is receiving social assistance, the amount of her social assistance would be reduced by $100.

Note: At the time of writing, this legislation was in effect in Vancouver and the Lower Mainland only, but it is proposed to be province wide by January 1, 1989.

h. CAN MY SPOUSE BOTHER ME WHEREVER I LIVE?

If you have moved out of the matrimonial home and established your own separate residence, your spouse has no right to be there, and there are legal grounds for having him or her ejected. In this case, the police will assist. They may not wish to interfere in such a domestic situation; but, if they are summoned and informed that the other spouse is trespassing, they should remove that person. Should they refuse to do so, it is possible to physically move to eject the other spouse under conditions of the Criminal Code of Canada.

Resistance by your spouse constitutes an assault and the police should step in to assist. However, this is a situation in which there may be violence, and the most extreme care should be taken to keep it to an absolute minimum. This should be attempted only in the presence of police officers.

i. WHAT SHOULD I DO IF MY SPOUSE ASSAULTS ME?

In some cases, the separation may be a violent one. If your spouse beats you or threatens your life or health, you should immediately telephone the police. Although the police hesitate to take an overly active role in matrimonial squabbles, frequently their very presence tends to subdue people. In cases of obvious physical danger, the police will interfere.

If you have suffered any injuries, even of a minor nature, you should see your family doctor or submit to examination in the emergency ward of a hospital. You should also have a friend or relative take photographs of the injuries, as these may be used as evidence against your spouse if court proceedings are started.

Finally, you could have your spouse charged for assault, threatening, or both. (This is discussed further in the next few pages.)

j. WHAT THE POLICE WILL (AND WON'T) DO

The police, even more than lawyers, dislike matrimonial disputes. They didn't become police to referee dish-throwing matches between angry couples. Usually they are called only as a last resort — when the parties are extremely hostile and emotions are boiling over. This is distasteful for any outsider and especially so for the police as most have had little or no training in handling this type of situation. The police in any confrontation of this nature are of limited help, and properly so. But there are situations where their intervention is necessary and very useful.

A sign in a local pizza parlor says that they have a deal with the local bank that the bank will not make pizzas and, in turn, they will not cash cheques. Similarly, you should not go to the police for legal advice. They do not wish to give it, and they are usually in no position to give it. In criminal matters, a good police officer knows as much law as most lawyers — and even more — but not in family matters. You will find fast, ready advice is merely a device to get you out of the station. And why not? The police have a function, and they should be called upon only in that capacity.

The basic duty of a police officer is to prevent breaches of the criminal law. This includes assaults, public disturbances, and breaking and entering. The police will come to quell violence and little else unless other laws are being broken. Where a hostile situation exists and there is a danger of violence, they will frequently urge one party or the other to leave for the night, or they will deliver a severe dressing down in the hopes of calming the situation.

If you find it necessary to telephone the police, tell them the problem, the offence being committed or feared, and ask them to come. Be brief, to the point, and businesslike. Do not attempt to involve them in the argument or expect them to take sides. They will be interested only in seeing that the law is obeyed and will not regard it as their function to give you or anybody else advice about rights. They will want only the facts.

k. THREATS, ASSAULTS, AND PEACE BONDS

The basic problems involving police concern assaults, threats, harassments, and so on. In these cases the police will intervene and possibly lay charges. Usually, however, you must give instructions before your spouse — or anyone else — will be charged with any of the different offences under the Criminal Code or other statutes. Some of the more usual sections of the Criminal Code invoked are shown below.

1. Assault

One person may not physically assault another and is liable to court prosecution if he or she is so unwise as to do so.

> Assault
>
> 244. A person commits an assault when, without the consent of another person or with consent, where it is obtained by fraud,
>
> > (a) he applies force intentionally to the person of the other, directly or indirectly, or
> >
> > (b) he attempts or threatens, by an act or gesture, to apply force to the person of the other, if he has or causes the other to believe upon reasonable grounds that he has present ability to effect his purpose.

Remember that the merest shove may be enough to constitute assault. The result of a conviction for a first offence would usually be a suspended sentence and a period of probation for a number of months. A term of the probation order would be that the accused have no contact with you, directly or indirectly. If you spouse breaches this term, he or she may be brought back to court and sentenced further or may be charged with breach of probation. The sentence for this would likely be a short period in custody. A deterrent, perhaps, equal to the threat of jail is the stigma of a criminal record.

If you wish to have your spouse charged, you should report the matter to the police. They will investigate the allegations and lay the charge. A popular misconception is that the assault victim does the charging. This is not so; the *state* makes the charge. Therefore, the victim does not have an automatic right to withdraw the charge if he or she subsequently decides not to proceed. The state (in the person of the prosecutor) may insist that the case go ahead.

The procedure is different if you want a peace bond under section 745 of the Criminal Code, which reads as follows:

> Any person who fears that another person will cause injury to him or his wife or child or will damage his property may lay an information before a justice.

The spouse requesting the peace bond should contact the police and have them investigate the concerns. The spouse must then attend in person to the provincial court and swear an information before a justice of the peace (J.P.). The J.P. will want to see a copy of the police investigation notes before this is done. From that point on, the procedure is the same as for an assault charge. The defendant will be summonsed to court and the judge will decide if there are reasonable grounds for the informant (the spouse who swore the information) to fear personal injury or property damage. If so, the defendant may be required to enter into a recognizance to keep the peace and be of good behavior for up to a year. If the defendant doesn't abide by this, he or she is guilty of a breach of recognizance and can be fined or sent to jail.

Whether the matter is an assault charge or an application for a peace bond, it will be handled in court by the prosecutor (a lawyer retained by the government), so it is not necessary for the victim to hire his or her own lawyer.

2. Intimidation

A third option in the Criminal Code is a charge of intimidation (section 381). One spouse may not intimidate another in an attempt to force him or her to do or not to do something. This often arises when parties are separated and one continually comes around to harass the other.

We have never seen this section used in a matrimonial matter, likely because of the provisions of the Family Relations Act which cover the same problem. Section 36.1 states that on application, a court —

> may make an order restraining any person from molesting, annoying, harassing, communicating, or attempting to communicate with the applicant or a child in the lawful custody of the applicant or both the applicant and a child.

If you wish to use this remedy, contact either a lawyer or family court counsellor who can assist you in making an application through family court.

l. CAN I WITHDRAW A CHARGE AGAINST MY SPOUSE?

As discussed earlier, the state, not you, lays the charge and so it is up to the prosecutor whether or not to withdraw the charge. You should be very reluctant to even make this request.

A charge should never be withdrawn merely because the person charged is attempting to frighten you. Should you give in to this form of pressure, you will never again be able to exert any control over that person as he or she will then know that any charges can ultimately be stopped. This will reinforce the impression that he or she can always win over you and you will end up in a worse position than you were in before.

In addition, should you withdraw a charge, you will have caused the court staff and police considerable work and effort for nothing, and you will lose your credibility with them. Consequently, should you find in a week or month's time that you again have to lay a charge, you will have difficulty getting help from them because you have already "cried wolf."

However, there are situations in which charges should be withdrawn. These are situations where proceeding with the charge would be a real detriment to the existing state of affairs. If the matrimonial situation is explained to the prosecutor — and how proceeding with the charges might interfere with the relationship — likely the prosecutor will agree to withdraw the charge.

m. LEAVE ME ALONE!

Often, once the parties have separated, or even while they are still living together, one harasses the other. One phones at all hours of the night and day, continually drives around the other's house, accosts him or her in the street or at work, continually comes into the home and generally makes life miserable. This type of situation can become extremely aggravating and often there is nothing that can be done about it, mainly because of the difficulties of compiling hard evidence that it is actually occurring.

If this happens to you, one obvious answer is for you to take up residence under an assumed name and to get an unlisted phone number. Calling the police can be effective to remove an obnoxious person from the front door, but usually nothing can be done about deep breathing exercises over the telephone at 3:00 in the morning.

When one of the spouses is living separately from the other and is maintaining his or her own residence, the other spouse has no right whatsoever because of the marital status to demand entrance into that residence.

Some husbands feel that even though they are living apart from their wives they can have sexual intercourse with them whenever they desire; but this is erroneous. The man may be charged with a sexual assault. In these situations the police should be called at the first opportunity. (See section i. above for further details.)

As mentioned, in these cases a wife can obtain a form of restraining order or injunction against her husband ordering him to cease harassing her. Problems like these should be discussed with a lawyer to see what solutions are available.

Evidence is always necessary in any of these matters, and you might be well advised to invest in a camera (preferably a Polaroid) and start taking photographs of the husband when he appears on the scene. Also, accurate notes should be kept of the time, date, and place of these episodes of harassment so that when the matter eventually ends up in court a very accurate record can be given by the complaining party.

If your spouse knows that you are taking these careful and detailed steps with the obvious intention of court proceedings, he or she will desist. Of course, if you are facing someone with a distorted mind, this type of tactic will not be a deterrent but will nevertheless by very useful when it comes time to give evidence in court.

3

DIVORCE AND ANNULMENT

When a marriage has broken down, usually a couple eventually wishes to dissolve their marital relationship. The marriage can be dissolved only if one or the other spouse has grounds for divorce or nullity. A new Divorce Act was proclaimed in 1985, which changed considerably the laws pertaining to divorce in Canada.

a. WHEN CAN I USE THE BRITISH COLUMBIA COURTS TO GET A DIVORCE?

To obtain a divorce in British Columbia, the following conditions must be met as of the date the proceedings for divorce are started:

(a) Either the husband or the wife has had his or her usual place of residence in British Columbia for a period of 12 months before the divorce proceedings were started;

(b) No proceedings have been started in any other province.

b. HOW LONG DOES A DIVORCE TAKE?

An uncomplicated divorce proceeding, that is, a divorce in which all outstanding matters with regard to children, maintenance, and property have been resolved or do not arise, usually takes approximately three months to complete in Vancouver. In areas outside Vancouver, the time may vary.

It is no longer necessary to have a court hearing for the granting of a divorce. You may simply file documents with the court registry and the court will process your divorce, provided it is uncontested.

The court will issue a divorce order, which may contain other orders (e.g., the maintenance and custody of children), provided there is something in writing indicating that the husband and wife consent to those orders being made. Thirty-one days after the pronouncement of the divorce order, the court will issue a certificate of divorce (providing a praecipe requesting the certificate has been filed), which means that the divorce is final. The husband and wife may not remarry during the 31-day waiting period. This period allows the parties to reopen the proceedings or appeal the order, and gives them a final opportunity to investigate the prospect of reconciliation. It is unusual to have a reconciliation at this stage, however. After the certificate of divorce has been issued by the court, the parties may each remarry someone else.

In cases in which the court feels there are special circumstances, it may make the divorce final at a time earlier than the thirty-first day after the judgment is rendered, provided that both the husband and the wife agree and undertake not to appeal the divorce order or to abandon any appeal from the divorce order. The court may fix the time when the divorce will take effect.

An uncontested divorce is one in which the husband and the wife have agreed on all outstanding matters between them, and there is nothing to fight over. Usually the divorce itself is not contested, but the husband and wife may not agree on who is to have custody of the children, how much access the non-custodial parent is to have to the children, or how much money the non-custodial parent is to pay for the maintenance of the other spouse and/or the children. In addition, the divorce petition may include a claim under the Family Relations Act for a division of family assets. The husband and the wife may not agree on what those assets are and how they should be divided. If any of these issues are not agreed upon, then the divorce becomes contested. The petitioning spouse (the petitioner) serves the divorce petition on the other spouse (the respondent), and the respondent files a document called an Answer to the Petition for Divorce. An Answer sets out the areas of concern to the respondent and in this manner the court is advised that the divorce is contested and a trial date must be set. The length of time it takes to obtain a trial in a contested divorce varies from place to place; however, it would probably be approximately one year.

When a divorce is uncontested, the petitioner serves the respondent with the Petition for Divorce, but the respondent does not file an Answer. The petitioner files an Affidavit giving the evidence on which the divorce is based. The Affidavit must show that reasonable arrangements have been made for the support of any children of the marriage. If the court is not satisfied that such arrangements have been made for the children of the marriage, it will not allow the divorce to proceed. The consent of the husband and wife to those arrangements is not necessarily sufficient to alleviate the court's concern about the children. Sufficient financial information must be filed so that the court can determine if the maintenance being paid for the support of the children is sufficient.

c. SUMMARY OF GROUNDS FOR DIVORCE

Under the new Divorce Act, which applies to all provinces including British Columbia, there is now only one ground for divorce: breakdown of a marriage. Breakdown of marriage can be established in one of three ways:

(a) If the husband and wife have lived separate and apart for at least one year immediately before the divorce is to be granted and if they were living separate and apart at the commencement of the divorce proceedings

(b) If the spouse against whom the divorce proceeding is brought has committed adultery

(c) If the spouse against whom the divorce is brought has treated the other spouse with physical or mental cruelty

1. Living separate and apart

To obtain a divorce on the ground of marriage breakdown based on living separate and apart for at least one year, the spouses must be living separate and apart at the time the divorce proceeding is started. Usually, in this case the husband and wife reside in separate residences. However, it sometimes happens that the husband and wife continue to live in the same home, but live entirely separate lives. To establish this, it may be shown that they do not cook for each other, clean for each other, eat together, or do any other thing that indicates they are living as husband and wife. All that is required to be proven is that there has been a complete withdrawal from the marital relationship with the intent to live separate and apart. The withdrawal can be by one spouse only, provided that spouse had the intent to live separate and apart.

On the other hand, it is not sufficient to show only a physical absence from one another. For example, a spouse may be hospitalized or serving in the armed forces or be abroad for a lengthy period of time visiting relatives, in which case the intention of destroying a matrimonial relationship is not present. Nor is it sufficient to show that no sexual intercourse took place if, at the same time, the spouses maintained a common household by sharing daily activities; however, prolonged refusal to have sexual relations may constitute cruelty.

As the philosophy of the Divorce Act is to encourage reconciliation, the parties may resume cohabitation for a period or periods totalling not more than 90 days, with reconciliation as its primary purpose, without breaking the one-year separation. In addition, if either the husband or the wife become incapable of forming or having an intention to continue to live separate and apart (e.g., if either spouse becomes mentally incompetent during the period of separation), and if it appears to the court that the separation would probably have continued if this spouse had not become so incapable, the one-year separation period is not considered to have been interrupted.

2. Adultery

To support a divorce action based on adultery, it is not necessary to show direct proof of an act of intercourse, since the court may infer adultery from circumstantial evidence combined with proof of familiarity and opportunity.

Rarely does a petitioner charging adultery come to a court equipped with photographs or films showing sexual intercourse. Most often the evidence would be the respondent's own admission that the adultery alleged in the divorce petition did, in fact, take place. Alternatively, the petitioner may call as a witness someone who can testify to something like the following:

> I saw the respondent and a woman (or man, as the case may be) enter a house at 10 p.m. I saw the bedroom light go out at 11 p.m. I marked the door and returned at 8 a.m. the following morning and ascertained that the respondent had not left the home.

An act of adultery need only occur once for it to be used as the basis for a divorce. It's important to realize that this is the case even though the parties are already separated and a formal separation agreement has been signed. Many feel that the standard clause in a separation agreement that says, in effect, "the parties are free to go their own ways and live their own lives," means they can commit adultery with impunity. Not so.

3. Cruelty

Cruelty is defined as conduct of such a nature as to render intolerable the continued cohabitation of the spouses. It may consist of physical abuse or mental torment. The definition allows for a wide scope of complaints but the conduct complained of must be of a grave and weighty nature. One act of cruelty is not sufficient; the conduct must have been continuous. Mere incompatibility is not legal cruelty.

The test of cruelty is a subjective one in that the court is primarily concerned with the effect the conduct has on the petitioning spouse. The husband who beats his wife or children illustrates a clear example of physical cruelty, but cruelty is not restricted to physical abuse; mental cruelty is just as valid a basis for divorce.

Where physical cruelty is relied on, the evidence must be clear and convincing to a court. It is, therefore, useful if a witness can testify that the spouse suffered a black eye, broken bones, or other physical injuries. If you are in this situation, it is always best to have a doctor examine and treat these injuries so that his or her report can be available at the trial. Evidence of immediate complaint of the incident to friends or relatives may also help establish physical cruelty.

On the other hand, if it can be shown that the conduct of one spouse has caused the other to suffer mentally or emotionally, or both, the court will usually accept such conduct as grounds for divorce. Some examples are wilful refusal to communicate over a long period of time, continual and entire nights away from home without cause or excuse, refusal to have sexual relations, continuous harsh and undue criticism, or denial of natural love and affection. In most instances involving mental cruelty, the wronged party consults a psychiatrist, marriage counsellor, or family doctor, or discusses the predicament with relatives or friends whose reports or testimony have a great influence on the court's decision to grant a divorce judgment.

d. BARS TO DIVORCE

Even when there is sufficient evidence to establish grounds for divorce, the court may, in some circumstances, refuse to grant a divorce judgment. There are four bars to divorce that have been incorporated into the Divorce Act:

1. Condonation

Condonation involves a resumption of cohabitation with the intention of forgiving the guilty spouse for his or her offensive conduct. It does not include, however, a continuation or resumption of cohabitation during any single period of less than 90 or multiple periods totally less than 90 days where such cohabitation is continued or resumed with reconciliation as the primary purpose.

2. Connivance

Connivance is an attempt by the petitioning spouse to encourage or persuade the other to commit a matrimonial offence in order to provide grounds for divorce.

3. Collusion

Collusion is a more serious matter in that the court is obliged to dismiss the petition if it finds that the conduct of either party is collusive. This does not mean that the parties cannot have entered into a separation agreement. Collusion means any action on your part to lie to the court or make up evidence so that you can get a divorce. In other words, your grounds must be legitimate, and when you go to court to testify on them, you must be telling the truth.

Both condonation and connivance are discretionary matters in that the court still has the power to grant a divorce if

71

it feels it is in the public interest to do so, despite one of the spouses being guilty of this conduct. Condonation and connivance are bars to a divorce only when the divorce is based on adultery or cruelty. They have no application to a divorce based on one-year separation.

4. Lack of support for children

The court may also refuse to grant a divorce if reasonable arrangements have not been made for the support of the children of the marriage and will only allow the divorce to proceed once those arrangements have been made.

e. ADDITIONAL REMEDIES

In conjunction with the divorce action, you may also claim for custody and maintenance of the children and maintenance for yourself. These issues are more fully dealt with in chapters 4 and 5. The advantage of having these issues dealt with by the judge hearing the divorce petition is that any orders he or she makes have legal effect throughout Canada, not only in British Columbia.

By means of a simple procedure, such an order may be registered in any province and be enforced as if it had been made in that province.

f. CAN I GET AN ANNULMENT?

This is a frequently asked question and, in most cases, the answer is no. An annulment means that the marriage has ceased to exist or has never existed at all in law. This is more than an academic consideration because of the tough jurisdictional problems that arise depending under which heading you fall. You should see a lawyer about it.

1. What are the grounds for annulment?

One ground for annulment is the lack of capacity to form a valid marriage. This may arise through a prior marriage, absence of consent to the marriage, mental incapacity that makes a party unable to understand the nature of the marriage ceremony, forbidden blood relationship, or just being too young. Each of these is a ground for annulment. Most of the cases in which a marriage is void arise because a prior marriage exists, and most of these are the result of bigamy.

Lack of consent may occur as a result of duress, fear, or fraud. But the ground for annulment that is currently in the news is the basic mistake or no real intention to get married. This has happened in cases where immigrants have married Canadians merely to get into the country. Some courts have held that as long as the parties understood the nature of the marriage (no matter what the reason for the marriage was), there can be no annulment. Such arrangements may be considered acts of dishonesty and the court may refuse to help.

Usually, in these cases the marriage has never been consummated, and you might think that you would be able to get an annulment or, after one year, a divorce. However, the courts have often refused to grant either an annulment or a divorce in these circumstances.

As annulment is a very complex area, a lawyer should be consulted. The best thing, however, is not to enter into a marriage of convenience at all.

Sexual impotence sufficient to obtain an annulment is the incurable inability or incapacity of one of the parties to have normal sexual intercourse with the other, and it must exist at the time of solemnization of the marriage. An annulment is not granted because the parties *don't* have sexual relations, but rather because they *can't*.

g. CHOOSING HOW TO PROCEED

Once you decide to proceed with divorce, you are then faced with the decision of whether or not to use a lawyer. The average uncontested divorce costs about $400 plus disbursements of roughly another $175. This is a great deal of money for a procedure that is basically simple and easy to do.

However, the complications that can arise are considerable, and to do a divorce yourself takes your time and effort, which can be saved by using a lawyer. Using a competent lawyer also avoids the possibility of falling into the pitfalls and errors that may cost you grief and heartache in the future. For instance, you may have property rights or rights concerning your children that you do not realize. Many of these rights are terminated upon a divorce. Moreover, if your grounds are shaky, you will be more certain of the outcome if you choose a competent lawyer. If you cannot afford to pay for a divorce, you should try to obtain legal aid.

If your situation is relatively simple and uncontested, you can certainly do it yourself by using the *Divorce Guide for British Columbia* and package of forms also published by Self-Counsel Press. The *Divorce Guide* sets out step by step what you must do to accomplish your task. Read the book and then decide what you wish to do.

You may also want to look into the many divorce services and divorce kits advertised. However, be very wary of the claims these services make and get a detailed accounting of the expenses and final cost to you. You may find the cost is not much less than going through with a lawyer of your choosing. (See chapter 7 for more information.)

If you decide to use a lawyer, you should be very careful to get a quote beforehand and arrange your finances accordingly. Most lawyers will allow you to pay a small retainer and make monthly deposits on that retainer so that, by the time the divorce is completed, your retainer has been built up to the full amount of the divorce fee. If one lawyer won't accept such terms, certainly the next one you talk to will; so give it a try. In some cases, too, you will be able to recover some of your costs from your spouse. Discuss this with your lawyer.

If there is more than a divorce involved or if your spouse is going to argue about maintenance, property, children, or in any way contest something, you may expect the fee to be much higher than that quoted above. In fact, the fee is likely to be so high that you and your spouse had best very seriously consider whether or not you want to fight it out in court. Discuss this with your lawyer and attempt to be very reasonable in your offers of settlement with your spouse as it is very much in your best interests to avoid a courtroom dispute.

h. PROCEDURE FOR AN UNCONTESTED DIVORCE

If you are using a lawyer, the initial step involves meeting with him or her. Make sure the lawyer is experienced in family matters (see chapter 7). The lawyer will question you on all the issues required for completion of the petition. From the information gathered, he or she will prepare the petition, have the action filed in the appropriate court, and then deliver copies of these documents to a process server who will then serve copies on the respondent(s).

If the respondents are served within British Columbia, they have 20 days in which to file an answer. If they are served in another Canadian province or in the United States, they have 40 days. Where service takes place in some other jurisdiction, the time limit is 60 days.

An answer is a document outlining the points in the divorce petition that are contested. If the requisite time period has expired and no answer has been filed, your lawyer may process the necessary documents to obtain your divorce order. The lawyer then files the following documents:

(a) Praecipe

(b) Affidavit of petitioner

(c) Registrar's certificate of pleadings;

(d) Affidavit of service of petition;

(e) Divorce order.

The affidavit is your evidence on the divorce and must be sworn before a lawyer. If your divorce is based on adultery or cruelty, other evidence may be necessary. The court will require, for example, for an uncontested divorce based on adultery, an affidavit and interrogatories from the respondent admitting the adultery. There may be medical evidence required for an uncontested divorce based cruelty. These pieces of evidence will be presented to the court by your lawyer when the rest of the documentation is submitted. After the court has had time to peruse the application for the divorce, provided it is prepared to grant the divorce, the divorce order is made. Thirty-one days later a certificate of divorce, which is a final formalization of the divorce, is issued, upon the filing of a praecipe requesting it. However, a final certificate of divorce is not issued if the respondent launches an appeal.

You cannot remarry until the final certificate of divorce is issued, so don't set a wedding date exactly 31 days from the day your divorce order is pronounced. You won't get it that quickly!

i. WHAT TO DO WHEN SERVED WITH A NOTICE OF PETITION AND PETITION FOR DIVORCE

These two documents together initiate a divorce proceeding (see Sample #6). When the process server hands you a copy of each of these documents, you may be asked to produce some form of identification such as a driver's licence or birth certificate. You should comply with these requests as they do not, in any way, amount to an admission of liability. By proving your identity, you are merely confirming that the right person has been served with the documents. (The usual practice in British Columbia is for the petitioner to provide the process server with a photograph of the respondent. This gives further confirmation that the person served is, in fact, the respondent.)

You will note from the notice of petition that you have a certain number of days within which to serve and file an answer and counter-petition.

An answer is delivered if you wish to dispute any claims that are made against you in the petition. If you wish to assert any affirmative claims against your spouse, you may also serve and file a counter-petition. Such claims may include a divorce itself based on any grounds that may be available to you, custody of or maintenance for your children, or maintenance for yourself.

If you fail to take any steps within the time period, you may well lose the privilege of contesting the divorce, or, in fact, of knowing when the divorce hearing takes place. Unless you are certain that you do not wish to have these privileges, you should take steps to retain a lawyer as soon as possible after you receive these documents, and, in any event, prior to the expiration of the time period.

j. CAN WE SUE FOR DIVORCE TOGETHER?

Under the new Divorce Act, a husband and wife can jointly petition for divorce, but only on the basis of one-year separation and only if nothing is asked for but the divorce. If one of the parties wishes custody or maintenance, a joint petition is not permitted unless those orders are consented to by the other spouse. Once the petition is filed, it need not be served. You should ensure that you have legal advice prior to entering into a joint petition, just as you would prior to commencing a petition for divorce or filing an answer. It is a very important legal document and you may have rights you are unaware of and that should be claimed in a petition for divorce.

k. WHAT NAME CAN A WIFE USE?

When a woman marries, she is entitled to continue to use her maiden name or, at her option, may legally use her husband's name. Even if she adopts her husband's name, she cannot legally be prevented from reverting to her maiden name at any time. (This has evolved from the principle that a person may use whatever name he or she chooses, as long as its use is not calculated to deceive or inflict pecuniary loss.)

Practically, however, it is usually difficult for a wife to convince appropriate authorities (e.g., passport office, motor vehicle licence bureau) to change her official documents to her maiden name without either a court order or a final divorce judgment.

After a divorce, a woman can revert to her maiden name, a right she has had all through her marriage. However, even if she has sole legal custody over the children, she cannot legally change their names to her maiden name without her husband's consent, although this consent can be waived by a judge of the Supreme Court.

The practical answer for a woman who does not have the money to hire a lawyer to make the application to the judge but who is considering reverting to her maiden name and knows that her husband will not consent to a change in their children's name is to simply allow the children to use her maiden name and instruct the teachers to call them by that name. When the children are 19 years of age, they can apply independently to formalize their name changes.

Court No. _____

Registry No. _____

IN THE SUPREME COURT OF BRITISH COLUMBIA

BETWEEN:

JOAN JONES

PETITIONER,

AND:

JOHN JONES

RESPONDENT(S)

Petition for Divorce

NOTICE TO: *(Name and address of each respondent and other person named in petition.)*

John Jones
73 Elsie Street
Vancouver, B.C.

Fanny Flirt
73 Elsie Street
Vancouver, B.C.

THIS IS A DIVORCE PROCEEDING. The claims made against you, or your alleged involvement in the breakdown of the marriage, are specified in this petition for divorce.

YOUR ATTENTION is directed to the **NOTICE AND DIRECTIONS TO PERSONS SERVED** which forms part of the petition and appears immediately after the signature of the petitioner.

The petition for divorce is issued out of the _Vancouver_ Registry of the Supreme Court of British Columbia on this _29th_ day of _December_, 19 8-.

Address of Registry:
(Full Address)
800 Smithe Street
Vancouver, B.C.
V6Z 2E1

_____
DISTRICT REGISTRAR

THIS IS THE PETITION FOR DIVORCE OF: *(Name and address of Petitioner.)*

Joan Jones
28 Hale Street
Vancouver, B.C.

CLAIM AND GROUNDS

(1) The petitioner claims a divorce from the respondent spouse (and, *add any claim for support, custody, costs or other relief claimed). (Attach additional pages as needed.)*
Custody and interim custody of the children of the marriage with reasonable access to the Respondent, maintenance and interim maintenance for the Petitioner and the children of the marriage, an Order pursuant to section 52 of the Family Relations Act and costs against the Respondent.

INTERNATIONAL SELF-COUNSEL PRESS LTD
1481 Charlotte Road
North Vancouver, British Columbia V7J 1H1
FORM CDN-D-BC (1-1) 87

(2) The petitioner alleges that there has been a breakdown of the marriage under the Divorce Act, 1985, section 8 (2) (a) (   ), [and section 8 (2) (b) (i), *as the case may be*] the particulars of which are as follows: (*Refer to specific paragraph(s) of section 8 (2) relied upon, and for particulars set out each material fact relied upon but not the evidence by which it might be proved.*)

The Petitioner and the Respondent will have lived separate and apart for at least one year immediately preceding the determination of the divorce proceeding and were living separate and apart at the commencment of the proceeding. The Respondent has committed adultery with the person named on numerous occasions from September, 198- to the present and has been living with the person named since September, 198- at 73 Elsie Street, Vancouver, B.C.

RECONCILIATION

(3) The particulars of the circumstances that may assist the court to determine if there is a possibility of the reconciliation of the spouses are as follows:

It is the position of the Petitioner that there is no possibility of reconciliation or resumption of cohabitation.

(4) The following efforts to reconcile have been made: (*Give particulars. If no effort has been made, state this.*)

No efforts to reconcile have been made.

PARTICULARS OF MARRIAGE

(5) Date of marriage: May 3, 1975

(6) Place of marriage: Vancouver, B.C.

(7) Surname of wife before marriage: White

(8) Maiden surname of wife: White

(9) Marital status of husband at time of marriage: Bachelor

(10) Marital status of wife at time of marriage: Spinster

(11) A certificate of the marriage or a certified copy of the registration of the marriage is filed with this petition (or, cannot be filed for the following reasons: [*state reason, e.g., all records destroyed by fire in marriage registry in country where marriage took place*]).

INTERNATIONAL SELF-COUNSEL PRESS LTD
1481 Charlotte Road
North Vancouver, British Columbia V7J 1H1
FORM CDN-D-BC (1-2) 87

RESIDENCE AND JURISDICTION

(12) Petitioner's residence is: 28 Hale Street
Vancouver, B.C.

(13) Respondent spouse's residence is: 73 Elsie Street
Vancouver, B.C.

(14) The petitioner and the respondent ceased to reside together on: August 27, 198-

(15) Petitioner's birth date: June 5, 1950

(16) Respondent's birth date: November 28, 1950

(17) Petitioner (or, The respondent spouse) has been ordinarily resident in British Columbia for at least one year immediately preceding the commencement of this proceeding.

AGE AND DISABILITY

(18) That no party or person named in this petition for divorce, excluding children of the marriage, is under 19 years of age except: *(name the person and give the age)*

(19) That no party or person named in this petition for divorce is under any other legal disability except: *(name the person and describe the disability)*

CHILDREN

(20) The name and date of birth of each living child of the marriage as defined by the Divorce Act, 1985 is:
Jonathan Jones, born April 3, 1980
Joanne Jones, born July 10, 1981

(21) The particulars of the past, present, and proposed custody, care, upbringing, and education of the child(ren) are as follows:
The children of the marriage have resided with the Petitioner since the parties separated and it is proposed that they remain in her custody.

INTERNATIONAL SELF-COUNSEL PRESS LTD
1481 Charlotte Road
North Vancouver, British Columbia V7J 1H1
FORM CDN-D-BC 11-31 87

(22) **The petitioner claims custody of the following child(ren):**

Jonathan Jones
Joanne Jones

(23) **The facts in support of the claim for custody are as follows:**

As stated above, the children have been in the care of the Petitioner since the parties separated and it would be disruptive to the children to uproot them at this time. The children are of tender years and the Petitioner feels she is in a better position to care for them, partly because she is not employed outside the hom whereas the Respondent is a long distance trucker and away a great deal.

(24) **The petitioner is willing for the respondent spouse to have access to the child(ren) as follows:** *(Give particulars, e.g., at all reasonable times, or every second weekend and one month during summer vacation. If petitioner objects to any access, state this and give reasons.)*

At all reasonable times, with reasonable notice.

OTHER PROCEEDINGS

(25) **The particulars and status of any other proceeding commenced with respect to the marriage or any child of the marriage, including proceedings for support or under any statute are as follows:** *(No proceeding prior to marriage, or adoption proceeding, should be included, but where a support order is in arrears, state the amount of arrears.)*

In October, 198-, the Petitioner obtained an order in Family Court pursuant to the Family Relations Act where the Respondent was required to pay the sum of $100 per month for the support of each of the children of the marriage, plus $200 per month for the support of the Petitioner.

SEPARATION AGREEMENTS AND FINANCIAL ARRANGEMENTS

(26) **The petitioner and the respondent spouse have entered into the following marriage agreement as defined in the Family Relations Act, or separation agreement, or other post or ante marriage agreement or financial arrangement:** *(Give particulars of dates and nature of each agreement and state whether or not it is still in effect.)*

There are no such agreements.

INTERNATIONAL SELF-COUNSEL PRESS LTD
1481 Charlotte Road
North Vancouver, British Columbia V7J 1H1
FORM CDN-D-BC (1-4) 87

(27) The financial position, both income and capital, of the petitioner and of the respondent is as follows: *(To be completed only if claim for support or custody, or other financial relief, is made.)*

The Petitioner is unemployed. Her only asset is a half interest in the matrimonial home located at 28 Hale Street, Vancouver, B.C.

The Respondent is a long distance trucker and earns a gross salary of $1,500 per month. Apart from the matrimonial home, he is the owner of a 1978 Cougar automobile and a small cabin on Green Lake, B.C., the values of which are unknown to the Petitioner.

COLLUSION, CONDONATION, AND CONNIVANCE

(28) There has been no collusion in relation to this petition, that is, there has been no agreement or conspiracy to which the petitioner is either directly or indirectly a party for the purpose of subverting the administration of justice, and no agreement, understanding or arrangement to fabricate or suppress evidence or to deceive the court.

(29) *(Where the ground for divorce is adultery or physical or mental cruelty).* There has been no condonation of or connivance at the grounds for divorce set forth in this petition. *(Or, where collusion or connivance exists, state the facts on which the court will be asked to find that the public interest would be better served by granting the divorce.)*

RELIEF CLAIMED

The Petitioner therefore claims and asks this Honourable Court to grant the following relief:

(a) that the petitioner and the respondent spouse shall be divorced from each other.

(b) Custody and interim custody of the children of the marriage with reasonable access to the Respondent

(c) Maintenance and interim maintenance for the Petitioner and the children of the marriage

(d) An order pursuant to section 52 of the Family Relations Act

(e) Costs against the Respondent

INTERNATIONAL SELF-COUNSEL PRESS LTD
1481 Charlotte Road
North Vancouver, British Columbia V7J 1H1
FORM CDN-D-BC (1-5) 87

PLACE OF HEARING

The Petitioner proposes that this petition will be heard by the Court at: *(place)* <u>Vancouver, B.C.</u>

SIGNED at <u>Vancouver</u> , in the Province of British Columbia, this day of <u>December 21</u> , 19 <u>8-</u> , the petitioner acknowledging that the statements in this petition for divorce are true to the best of the petitioner's knowledge, information and belief.

<u>Joan Jones</u>
Signature of Petitioner

Petitioner's address for service/delivery: *(must be within 10 miles [16 km] of the registry)*

Petitioner's telephone number:

INTERNATIONAL SELF-COUNSEL PRESS LTD.
1481 Charlotte Road
North Vancouver, British Columbia V7J 1H1
FORM CDN-D-BC (1-6) 87

NOTICE AND DIRECTIONS
TO PERSONS SERVED

LET ALL RESPONDENTS and other persons upon whom this petition for divorce is served TAKE NOTICE:

(a) If you wish to oppose the divorce proceeding or any claim made against you, or if you wish to advance claims of your own, you must cause a document known as an "Answer" or an "Answer and Counterpetition," respectively, in the form prescribed by the Rules of Court to be filed in the above noted registry of this court and cause a copy to be either delivered or served, as provided by the Rules, on the petitioner or, if the petitioner has a lawyer, delivered to that lawyer, within the following time limit:

    (i) If YOU were within BRITISH COLUMBIA when served with this petition for divorce, the time limit is TWENTY (20) DAYS; or

    (ii) If YOU were anywhere else in CANADA or in one of the continental UNITED STATES OF AMERICA when served, the time limit is FORTY (40) DAYS; or

    (iii) If YOU were served anywhere else, the time limit is SIXTY (60) DAYS, and

    (iv) If the petition for divorce was served upon you by some substitutional means (not in person) the time limit is the time fixed by the order of this court granting substituted service.

(b) Your Answer, or Answer and Counterpetition, must provide an address at which further documents may be served or delivered, which address, unless it is the office address in British Columbia of your lawyer, must be within 10 miles (16 kilometres) of the above noted registry of this court,

(c) If you do not file and serve or deliver an Answer or Answer and Counterpetition within the proper time limit set out above, then the petitioner may proceed WITHOUT ANY FURTHER NOTICE TO YOU, you will not be entitled to further notice, and a judgment granting a divorce and any other claims against you may be given IN YOUR ABSENCE,

(d) THAT, unless the court otherwise orders, a divorce takes effect on the 31st day after the day on which the judgment granting the divorce is rendered, AND THAT neither spouse is free to remarry until the divorce is in effect,

(e) If you are not a respondent but have been named in the petition for divorce and you wish to make a claim against the petitioner for costs or other relief, you must apply to the court to be added as a respondent within the time limit set out above and the court will decide the additional time, if any, to be given you for the purpose of filing an Answer or Answer and Counterpetition.

INTERNATIONAL SELF-COUNSEL PRESS LTD
1481 Charlotte Road
North Vancouver, British Columbia V7J 1H1
FORM CDN-D-BC (1-7) 87

4
MAINTENANCE AND SUPPORT BETWEEN HUSBAND AND WIFE

a. SUPPORT GENERALLY

Historically, the law required a man to maintain his wife. But times have changed and the conditions that gave rise to this no longer exist. It is not uncommon now for a wife to support the family or contribute substantially to the family income. Under the Divorce Act, and under the Family Relations Act, a husband can now seek support from his wife.

There are three sources of authority for one spouse seeking support from the other. The first is the simple law of contract, that is a separation agreement. If husband and wife agree on an amount of support and write it into the agreement, it is as enforceable as any other contract. Payments not made remain owed, and one can take the other to court to recover the debt.

The second source of authority is the power given to the court under the Divorce Act to award maintenance on a divorce. This, of course, applies only to a formal marriage situation and the application should be made at the time of the divorce.

The third source of authority is found under Part 4 of the Family Relations Act.

b. PRIOR TO DIVORCE

1. Your claim for support

If a couple have separated amicably and agree on how much money should be paid for support, they can include a term to that effect in a written separation agreement. Frequently, however, couples cannot agree. In many cases, one feels the other is entitled to nothing. You may not be able to obtain a divorce or may not wish one, but you still have the right to apply to the courts for support.

Under Part 4 of the Family Relations Act, either a husband or a wife or a common-law spouse who has cohabited with a partner for two years may apply for support. In determining liability to pay support, the act sets forth several criteria to consider:

(a) The role of each spouse in the family

(b) An express or implied agreement between the spouses that one has the responsibility to support and maintain the other

(c) Custodial obligations respecting a child

(d) The ability and capacity of and the reasonable efforts made by either or both spouses to support themselves

(e) Economic circumstances

Except as provided above, the act requires a spouse to be self-sufficient.

2. How much will you receive?

In determining the amount of support, the court considers the assets and means of each of you and any benefit or loss of benefit under a pension plan or annuity. Your capacity to provide for your own support is taken into account. You cannot simply sit at home for no reason at all, refuse to work, and expect to get support from your spouse.

Your spouse's capacity is also considered. Age and physical and mental health of both of you are taken into account. If you have lived together for a relatively short time, it is not likely that one has acquired a financial dependence on the other and, therefore, the amount of support may be little or none at all.

In determining how much support should be paid, the court looks at the accustomed standard of living of both of you. If there is enough money available, the court tries to insure that the dependent spouse can continue to lead a style of life as close as possible to the style that had been enjoyed prior to the separation.

The court also looks at the means available for the dependent spouse to become financially independent and the costs involved. If, for example, you haven't worked for a considerable length of time, you may have to take some kind of retraining, whether it be to brush up on your skills or to learn about the latest developments in your career. However, if it is desirable for you to stay home and take care of a young child, the court may feel that you should not retrain at this time and that you are not in a position to be earning income.

If it is a second marriage, one or the other of you may have an obligation to support a child or spouse from a former marriage. This factor may affect the amount that is available to provide for the new spouse, and the court will take this into account.

You may have married while in university. Your spouse might have pursued his or her studies in law, engineering, or medicine while you were out working. You may have quit school and given up your ability to engage in a meaningful career in order to maintain the financial viability of the family during those difficult and hard times. In these circumstances, the court may frequently give you a higher periodic payment or even a lump sum to compensate you for these efforts.

3. What entitles you to support?

As previously stated, the way you have treated each other is disregarded in establishing an obligation to provide support. Before the passage of the Family Relations Act, a wife could only obtain support from her husband if she had "grounds" — if she could prove he had committed adultery, had treated her with cruelty, had deserted her, or had failed to provide reasonable support and maintenance for her.

To prove these grounds, the wife usually had to wash all her dirty laundry in public. The husband could then defend the proceeding by showing that the wife had committed adultery or cruelty or had deserted him. Frequently, he would present evidence about every tiny little transgression of the wife over the course of the whole marriage. This was a disgusting, undesirable state of affairs!

It is no longer necessary to go into all these details of day-to-day life in a marriage in order to get support. The only criterion is need. If you need support, the court, after examining all the circumstances mentioned here, will give you a support award against your spouse.

4. Where to apply

An application for support under the Family Relations Act can be brought either in the provincial court, family division (family court), or in the Supreme Court of British Columbia. If your case is relatively simple, you can bring the application for support yourself in family court. In Supreme Court, however, the procedure is more complicated and you would be wise to retain a lawyer.

The family court facility is best used in circumstances where the family is in a relatively low income bracket or where the financial position of the parties is relatively simple. A complex financial situation usually necessitates some form of pre-trial investigation, which cannot be done in the family court procedure. However, the act does contain a provision (applicable both to family court and Supreme Court) that requires a party, on request in writing, to provide the other party with copies of current or relevant income tax returns and assessment notices, itemized statements of revenue and expenses, and itemized statements of assets and liabilities. However, the family court, unlike the Supreme Court, has no procedure similar to an examination for discovery to allow some searching questions about the financial material provided. Those questions have to wait until you are actually in the courtroom.

If you wish an order concerning real property, the family court has no jurisdiction to make it. In that circumstance, the application must be brought to the Supreme Court. This procedure require that you hire a lawyer.

If you feel the family court is appropriate to deal with your situation, you should contact the court in your area to inquire about making an application. In most areas in British Columbia, the court staff — usually family court counsellors — are trained to assist you in making your application. They also take the necessary steps to have your spouse served with the application and arrange to bring the matter before the judge.

5. Powers of the court

Under the Family Relations Act, the courts can order the following types of support:

(a) A periodic payment (i.e., a sum of money on a monthly or yearly basis)

(b) A lump sum payment either to be paid or held in trust under whatever terms and conditions the court orders

(c) That property be charged with payment under the order

An order for support can now be retroactive to the date the application in the proceeding was served on the respondent. It can also be changed by the court at any time if your financial circumstances change. This necessitates further application to the court and usually a lawyer should be consulted.

If you have a written separation agreement in which you have agreed not to sue for support, the court may feel itself bound by the agreement, unless the provisions for support set out in the agreement are unconscionable, the applicant qualifies for welfare assistance, or the person obliged to provide support is in default under the agreement.

At the same time that you seek support, you can claim support for the children and apply to have the court determine the division of property. Only the Supreme Court can deal with the property issue so if there is any argument about property, probably your claim for support should also be made at the Supreme Court. Otherwise you will have two different courts dealing with matters that are intertwined. For example, the amount of support to be awarded to a spouse will vary depending on whether or not that spouse was awarded the matrimonial home.

If subsequently you are divorced, a support order under the Family Relations Act continues in full force and effect unless the divorce court has dealt with the question of support. In that case, the support order under the divorce will govern.

c. DIVORCE PROCEEDINGS

When your divorce comes to trial, the court can also deal with the issue of support. When determining support, it considers the same criteria as set out in the Family Relations Act. The Divorce Act also specifies the objectives of an order for the support of a spouse. An order should —

(a) recognize any economic advantages or disadvantages to the spouses arising from the marriage or its breakdown

(b) apportion between the spouses any financial consequences arising from the care of any child of the marriage

(c) relieve any economic hardship of the spouses arising from the breakdown of the marriage

(d) as much as is practicable, promote the economic self-sufficiency of each spouse within a reasonable period of time

The Divorce Act, like the Family Relations Act, is clear that the court is not to take into consideration any misconduct of a spouse in relation to the marriage. Further, the comments made earlier regarding the effect of a separation agreement and the possibility of varying a support order under the Family Relations Act apply equally to orders under the Divorce Act.

d. INTERIM SUPPORT

A support action or divorce proceeding may take a year or longer to reach the point of trial. Often, you cannot wait until the final disposition of the trial; you need funds to maintain yourself during this time. Simultaneously with the beginning of the litigation, you can make a summary application for what is known as "interim support."

On this type of application, the court examines your need and expenses and your spouse's ability to pay and awards an interim sum to enable you to live modestly pending the trial.

e. IF YOUR SPOUSE DOESN'T PAY, HOW CAN YOU ENFORCE PAYMENT?

On September 1, 1988, new legislation, entitled the Family Maintenance Enforcement Act, was passed to assist spouse to enforce an order for maintenance, basically by taking all the "hassle" out of their hands. The "creditor" (the spouse entitled to receive maintenance) may register the order for support with a provincial government body called the Maintenance Enforcement Program. The "debtor" (the spouse required to pay support) would then be notified to send the maintenance payments to the program to be forwarded to the creditor. The program then monitors the situation to ensure payments are kept up to date.

The director of the program has wide access to information about the debtor that assists in enforcing payment. He has the right to demand from any person or public body, including the Crown, information regarding the debtor's place of employment, the location of assets, and the sources of income. If a payment is missed, the director can require the debtor to file a statement of finances. If the debtor fails to do so within the prescribed time, he or she may be ordered to pay up to $5 000 to the creditor spouse and may also face imprisonment up to 30 days.

If a spouse is in arrears, the director can attach or garnishee money due and owing the debtor. Normally, this involves ordering the debtor's employer to send a portion of his or her salary directly to the creditor. The defaulting spouse can also be summonsed to court to "show cause" as to why he or she is in arrears. If the judge is satisfied that the debtor is able to pay the arrears, he or she may order that the money be paid by a particular date or paid in monthly instalments over and above the regular maintenance payment. If these payments aren't made, the court may order a jail sentence of up to 30 days for each payment missed. Spending time in jail does *not* cancel the money owing.

Another remedy available is to obtain a warrant of execution from the provincial court that will allow the sheriff to seize the debtor's furnishings, car, or other eligible assets.

An order for maintenance may be filed in the Land Title Office and would prevent your spouse from dealing in any way with property registered in the spouse's name. This puts you in a position of strength. For example, if your spouse wished to sell the property, you could agree to withdraw the order provided that the existing arrears were paid and some other security substituted to ensure future payments. If you spouse did not wish to sell but was behind in maintenance payments, you could apply to the court to force the sale in order to satisfy your judgment.

These remedies are available to the creditor whether or not he or she chooses to use the Maintenance Enforcement Program, but the program does have access to information and counsel available to pursue the debtor. If you have further questions about this program, you may call 660-3281 if you live in the Greater Vancouver area or 1-800-663-9666 if you live elsewhere in the province.

f.   WHAT IF MY SPOUSE LIVES OUT OF THE AREA?

The Family Relations Act contains provisions that allow the court to award maintenance or enforce an existing order for maintenance even when your spouse does not live in British Columbia. All the provinces plus many of the American states and other foreign countries have "reciprocal legislation" that allows maintenance orders made in one jurisdiction to be confirmed and enforced in another.

The following jurisdictions have reciprocal agreements with British Columbia:

(a) All of the provinces and territories of Canada

(b) These states of the United States:

California	Kansas
Colorado	Maine
Connecticut	Michigan
Idaho	Minnesota
Montana	Ohio
Nebraska	Oregon
Nevada	Pennsylvania
New Hampshire	Vermont
New Mexico	Virginia
New York	Washington
North Dakota	Wisconsin

(c) In Africa:

Republic of South Africa	Zimbabwe

(d) In Europe:

Austria	Gibraltar
United Kingdom	Isle of Man
Bailiwick of Guernsey	Norway
Federal Republic of Germany (including Land Berlin)	
States of Jersey	

(e) In the South Pacific:

Australian Capital Territory	South Australia
Fiji	Tasmania
Northern Territory of Australia	Victoria
New South Wales	Western Australia
New Zealand	
Queensland	
Territory of Papua and New Guinea (including Cook Island)	

(f) In Asia:
     Hong Kong   Singapore

To apply for maintenance, you may contact the provincial court (family court) directly. Arrangements are then made for you to testify in court as to your financial situation and anything you know about your spouse's. The judge, on the basis of your evidence alone, makes what is called a — provisional order— for maintenance. A transcript of your evidence plus the provisional order is then forwarded to the jurisdiction where your spouse is residing. He or she will be summonsed to the court closest to his or her place of residence. After hearing the evidence regarding your spouse's financial situation and reading the transcript of your evidence that you gave in the British Columbia court, the judge will either confirm the provisional order or vary it.

If you already have a final maintenance order "either made under the Family Relations Act or the Divorce Act" and your spouse has fallen into arrears, the reciprocal legislation allows the court in the area where your spouse lives to enforce the order in the same manner as if he or she were living in British Columbia. There is no point to such an application if you cannot say exactly where your spouse is living. In that case, you may need to employ the services of a skip-tracer.

5
CHILDREN

a. THE CUSTODY OF CHILDREN GENERALLY

It is over the custody of children that the most bitter family disputes rage; and the innocent children stand in the middle, suffering greatly as a consequence. In these matters, remember always that the children are usually loyal to both parents and do not have the bitterness and hatred that each parent relies on as protection against hurt.

Parents embroiled in such disputes should do everything possible not to draw the children into the fray and in particular not to use them as pawns in the game of matrimonial chess. The fight should take place out of the presence of the children; when they are present each parent should honor the other. The children, too, have certain rights, and one of these rights is to have the opportunity to have a relationship with both parents.

Until the court says otherwise, parents have equal rights to the custody of children. As a result, it is often tempting for one parent to take the matter of custody into his or her own hands and physically snatch the children away from the parent with actual custody. Except in very severe circumstances, this is not usually in the best interests of the children and it seldom solves any problems. The proper way to resolve a dispute over custody is either to reach an agreement or to apply to the proper court (see the following for description of the various courts).

1. Jurisdiction of the courts

Generally speaking, in order for a court to exercise jurisdiction over the children, the children must be physically within that jurisdiction, and for this reason, prior to the court granting custody to one parent or the other, it is important to see that the children are not removed from the province.

In cases in which the removal of children is threatened out of malice or in an attempt to avoid a court disposition, the courts will grant an order to the effect that the children not leave the province. Should you disobey this order, you would be in contempt of court and subject to fine or imprisonment. Of course, once a custody order is made, it is permissible to take the children out of the province unless the court has ordered that they not be removed from the jurisdiction. If such a clause has been made part of the custody order and you disobey it, you would be in contempt of court and subject to a fine or imprisonment.

When custody matters are before the courts, the judge disregards the feelings and rights of both parents and looks solely to the interests of the child. What is in the best interests of the child is the paramount issue. This takes precedence over any "rights" of the natural parents. Suppose, for example, that a child had been placed with a grandmother or family friend and lived with that person for several years. Then the parents decided to retrieve custody. The court might well order that the child remain where he or she is in preference to the parents if that seemed to be in the child's best interest.

The "best interest test" is also applied in determining custody of an "illegitimate" child. In the past, when a child was born out of wedlock, the mother used to have the absolute right to control the custody of the child, and the father, in law, had no rights. Gradually, the father, under the law, acquired the right to obtain custody if the mother was unfit. Now the courts have shifted their focus to the child and will award custody in accordance with his or her best interests. Neither parent stands on a better footing than the other.

A mother who commits adultery does *not* disentitle herself to custody. The court does not assume an unfaithful wife constitutes an unfit mother unless such conduct affects the well-being of the child (such as prostitution). Again, the welfare of the child is the only interest.

2. Discrimination against fathers

Many fathers have been known to complain that custody is one area in which the law discriminates against men in favor of women. To some extent this is true, particularly with regard to infants. The courts generally follow the principle that children of "tender years" are best off with their mothers. As roles in society change, however, so too do the legal principles. In many couples, the woman really isn't in any better position than her spouse to take on the full parenting responsibility.

Statistically, in by far the majority of cases, the mother has custody. However, this is usually a situation reached by agreement between the parties when they separate and it acknowledges that in their particular relationship the mother did play the primary parenting role. Looking only at the cases where custody has been determined by the court, particularly in the case of older children (say seven and up), fathers are succeeding in close to half of the battles.

3. Changing the custody award

With the matter of custody of children, the situation is never a closed book. It may always be brought back before the courts for further review. As a result, if one parent has the custody of the children and for some reason the situation is not working out well, the other parent may return to court and seek custody. This may occur years after the matter of custody was originally "settled." And the courts would simply look again to what is in the best interests of the children.

4. Visitation rights

A child has a right to a relationship with both parents, even though they can't get along with each other. Further, the older the child, the more his or her wishes are considered, and most judges consider it best for the child to be seeing both parents. As a result, a court will almost always couple a custody order with the right to access for the other parent.

The usual order is for reasonable access, and it is left up to the parties to arrange the visits between themselves, hopefully in the best interests of the child, which means a regular arrangement in which the child can visit the other parent. Normally the child and visiting parent should spend the day together out of the child's home as this is usually the easiest and most desirable arrangement for all parties concerned and reduces the tension and problems that may occur during a visit. Don't, whatever you do, let your bitterness or hatred spoil your child's right to have a good and lasting relationship with his or her other parent.

If you sincerely feel that it is not in the child's best interests to see the other parent, then you may refuse access, but at the risk of some judge in the future levelling a verbal blast at you for your actions. If possible, you should return to the court to ask for an order excluding access and explain your reasons for doing so.

5. Factors affecting custody awards

To briefly summarize then, the principles affecting custody are as follows:

(a) The welfare of the child is paramount.

(b) The court considers the opinion of older children. Fights for custody of teenagers are rare because you can't really force a child of that age to live where he or she doesn't want to.

(d) Siblings are almost always kept together.

As mentioned, full-blown custody fights are probably the messiest of legal actions. It is much better for you to agree on custody and keep relations between you and your "ex" relatively civil.

6. Joint custody

The ultimate in civil relations between spouses — and certainly tremendous for the children *when it works* — is to do away with the whole notion of "ownership" ("*I* have custody — the kids are *mine.*")) and agree to share custody. This necessitates both parents *agreeing* to such an arrangement; the court rarely orders it unless both want it that way. And the parents must be able to communicate with each other so that there is consistency for the children regardless of which parent they are with at a particular time.

The mechanics of joint custody vary. If the parents reside in the same area, the children may spend a few months with mom, then a few months with dad, the close proximity allowing them to continue at the same school with the same set of neighborhood friends. Or the children may remain in the same house while the parents take turns living there with them. Or the parties may acknowledge that one parent is the "parent in residence" but the other parent plays a far fuller role than merely visiting the children every other weekend. If it works, great. More and more couples seem to be making this type of arrangement, again reflecting the more active parenting role that fathers are now playing.

b. HOW TO GET CUSTODY

1. By agreement

When you enter into a separation agreement, the matter of custody of children can be covered in the agreement. The agreement in Sample #4 includes sample clauses for this purpose.

The courts always reserve the right to review the matter of custody and maintenance and, should the spouse without custody under the agreement decide to challenge the agreement, he or she can bring it before the courts very quickly. However, that spouse would be faced with the difficulty of convincing a judge that, once having decided to give them up, he or she should now have the children. The courts step in where the best interests of the children seem to dictate that that be done.

A separation agreement is a very useful document for the spouses because it not only sets out the voluntary arrangement but has evidentiary value as to the fitness and propriety of the parent who is to have the children. The fact that it can be challenged in court should not discourage you from entering into a separation agreement if initial agreement is possible.

2. By court application

(a) Family Relations Act

The act allows an application to be made either to the Supreme Court or to provincial court — either independently or joined with a claim for other relief such as maintenance.

As stated, the principle followed in determining custody is the best interests of the child. The act sets out certain criteria to be considered in making this determination:

(a) The health and emotional well-being of the child including any special needs for care and treatment

(b) Where appropriate, the views of the child

(c) The love, affection, and similar ties that exist between the child and other persons

(d) Education and training for the child

(e) The capacity of each person to whom guardianship, custody, or access rights and duties may be granted to exercise these rights and duties adequately

(b) Divorce Act

A claim for custody is commonly part of the divorce action and either husband or wife can initiate the action. Divorce hearings come under the jurisdiction of the Supreme Court and, using the power of this court, the judge can award custody even though the divorce application is unsuccessful (see chapter 3 for an explanation of divorce procedure).

c. RIGHTS OF ACCESS

Rights of access refer to visiting rights awarded a parent when the other parent has custody of the children. The occasions and frequency of access are usually arrived at by agreement between the spouses. Times are arranged that are mutually convenient and beneficial to the children.

As a matter of practice, rights of access are almost always granted because the courts feel it is a *right* of a child, and in his or her best interest, to have a continuing relationship with both parents. The exception would be if it could be shown that the visits have a detrimental effect on the child, that there is a real danger of physical or emotional harm, or that a parent has deserted the child by not communicating over a long period of time.

"Reasonable access" should be worked out between the parties. Failing this, the courts will impose a schedule which usually means that the person without custody would be entitled to access on weekends and/or during certain holiday periods — especially the summer holidays.

If the parents are at each other's throats, any contact between them, at least at the beginning of the separation, is bitter and temptation is great to use the children for one or the other's advantage. Fortunately, over time, as emotions change and understanding grows, the situation usually improves. If it doesn't, the non-custodial parent may find it virtually impossible to enforce the access order. If the parent with custody is flagrantly refusing to allow the child to visit, that parent may be found in contempt of court and penalized. More common, however, and much harder to deal with, is the more subtle custodial parent who brainwashes the child either deliberately or unconsciously, so that the child doesn't want to visit. Technically the non-custodial parent could enforce the access order by having the child picked up bodily by the police and delivered to his or her place of residence — but it's not likely to be an enjoyable visit! There are some extreme cases where, regrettably, it's in the child's best interest that there be no access so the child isn't subjected to the constant conflict. One can only hope that some time down the road the parent and child can pick up the pieces and form a relationship.

Note that failure to pay child support does not in itself constitute grounds to refuse access. The two matters are treated separately by the court. If the non-custodial parent obviously has the means to pay support and has refused to do so, the court may feel that this is tantamount to deserting the child and access should be denied. If, however, the parent has failed to meet his or her maintenance obligations because of financial hard times, it's likely that the court would still encourage access to take place.

If you have an order for access and visiting rights are being refused, you may want to consult a professional who specializes in family mediation. But if mediation fails, you may turn to the courts for assistance in enforcing the order. Section 81(2) of the Family Relations Act —

> A person who, without lawful excuse, interferes with the custody of, or access to, a child in respect of whom an order for custody or access was made or is enforceable under this act commits an offence.

Thus, you can go to the nearest provincial court and ask that your spouse be charged with an offence if access is being denied. You do not need to hire your own lawyer to take this matter to court: the Crown counsel would prosecute the case, just as if it were a criminal matter. If convicted, your spouse could face a term of imprisonment. In most cases, however, at least for a first offence, the court would likely impose a period of probation. The offending spouse would have the threat of jail hanging over him or her if there were any further denials of access.

This procedure is more difficult if your access order reads "reasonable access" rather than sets out specific terms because the spouse with custody could argue that the visits he or she was allowing *were* reasonable and that you were being unreasonable for wanting more. So you may be looking at a two-part process: first, get your access order varied so the terms of visits are set specifically; then, if access continues to be a problem, consider charging your spouse with an offence.

Note: Laying charges should be a last resort. Parents who are at war with each other are not likely to serve the child's best interests.

d. ASSISTANCE IN RESOLVING THE ISSUES OF CUSTODY AND ACCESS

As mentioned, custody cases can be the worst of legal battles and the parents should be urged to avail themselves of whatever conciliation services may be available.

Family court counsellors (or conciliation counsellors) are attached to both the provincial (family) court and the Supreme Court. They are experienced in assisting parties to resolve custody disputes. In addition, there are some well-qualified people in private practice with agencies not attached to the court, and their services may be well worth retaining.

So even if legal proceedings have been started, it's not too late to avoid the courtroom. The court will often order that a custody report be prepared by someone such as the conciliation counsellor or social worker. If the report is well done, it may be abundantly clear where the child should be. In some cases the Attorney General's office may appoint a family advocate to represent the child's best interests in a custody case.

A family advocate is basically the child's lawyer and has the advantage of objectivity, not having to follow instructions from one or the other of the parents. After meeting with the child and speaking with people who have had an opportunity to observe him or her, such as the school teacher, family doctor, etc., the picture may be clear. The family advocate can then meet with both parties and their respective counsel and advise what position he or she will be taking on behalf of the child and why. And again, even at this late stage, the courtroom confrontation may be avoided.

If the matter is not resolved out of court, the family advocate plays an active role in the court proceedings, often calling independent witnesses to testify on behalf of the child's interests. The court is likely to place more weight on the evidence of these persons than those called by either parent. For example, the evidence of a psychiatrist retained and paid by one parent (who often has not even laid eyes on the other parent) is not going to be viewed as being as objective as the evidence of a psychiatrist retained by the family advocate who has had an opportunity to meet with and assess all the parties.

The government policy on the appointment of a family advocate is vague. The broad guideline is that a family advocate will not be appointed for a child over the age of 12; nor will one be appointed in a matter arising under the Family and Child Services Act unless there are extenuating circumstances. But exceptions are made. If you are involved in a situation in which you feel a child needs separate representation (either in a custody battle or a case of abuse or neglect), have your lawyer phone Victoria (384-4434) and speak to the person in charge to determine whether the government will agree to make such an appointment.

e. SHOULD I JUST TAKE MY CHILD?

As it has already been pointed out, until the court orders otherwise, both parents, married or in a common-law union, have equal rights of custody. However, it would appear that the parent with the actual or "de facto" custody is the one with the prior legal right, at least until a court orders otherwise.

What sometimes happens is that one parent, the one without the custody of the children, will, for one reason or another, decide to take custody without the benefit of a court order and merely show up on the spouse's doorstep and remove the children or fail to return the children after a visit. This is frequently termed "child snatching." However, it is a cruel and harsh step to take and it is seldom in the best interests of the children because it usually arises when one spouse or the other is attempting to use the children as a pawn in a game of "get the other."

There may be situations where such action is justified, for example, where the children are not being looked after properly. However, a court action for an order for custody should be brought first. If the children are in serious need of protection and are living in a dangerous situation, the matter should be reported to the Superintendent of Family and Child Service who should be asked to intervene and take the children out of the home.

Should you find yourself in a situation where the children have been snatched, you can go immediately to court using one of the methods described and seek an interim order for return of the children and for custody. Such an application is usually very complex and legal advice should be sought.

Sometimes, the court will make an order for the return of the child without your spouse even having notice of the application. This order lasts for a short period of time until you have had an opportunity to notify your spouse. It is important that these orders contain specific directions to law enforcement authorities to assist in obtaining custody of the child. Otherwise, you might find it difficult to have the police or the RCMP assist you.

f. CAN I JUST TAKE THE CHILDREN AND LEAVE THE PROVINCE OR COUNTRY?

The answer is yes, you probably can, but you should not. Why? First, your spouse would still likely obtain an order for custody and it is possible to have this order enforced in another province; and if you are ever brought before a judge — look out!

In addition, there is nothing to stop your "ex" from moving to the new province and obtaining a new order that could be enforced quite easily.

The last and the most important consideration is the effect on the children; you will have to conclude there is little to be gained from such a move.

The law in this area is very technical and complex. As a general statement while the courts may make a custody order for children who have been taken from the province on the grounds that they are ordinarily resident in British Columbia, the problems of enforcing the order are considerable and expensive.

If you are concerned that the person without legal custody might take the children and run, you may apply to the court for an order restraining your spouse from removing them from the province. Breaching such an order would leave the offending spouse subject to penalty for contempt of court. Also the court in the jurisdiction to which the offending spouse goes would be more likely to refuse to deal with the matter and direct that the children be returned to British Columbia because of the existence of an order there.

To summarize, contempt of the courts of this province would be likely to show the person contemptuous of all courts and thus render his or her reception in the court of another jurisdiction less favorable.

When dealing with orders made in another jurisdiction we are in an area of law called "conflicts of law" or sometimes "private international law," and it is a very specialized and complicated area. As mentioned, the advice of a lawyer must be sought immediately.

g. CUSTODY WHEN A PARENT DIES

If the parents were living together or were separated and had agreed to joint custody, then the child would continue in the custody of the surviving parent. If the parents were separated and the custodial parent died, the survivor would not automatically have custody. For example, if the custodial parent had a will designating someone else as guardian, that person would assume custody. The surviving parent would certainly have an opportunity to challenge this in court, and the decision would be based, not on his or her rights as a parent, but rather on what appeared to be in the child's best interest.

h. MUST MY SPOUSE SUPPORT OUR CHILDREN?

When dealing with children, the court is always be concerned that they are adequately maintained. The obligation to maintain children financially falls on both parents. This obligation continues even if the spouse with custody remarries. For example, as often happens, the wife remarries and the "ex" feels he can stop payments to the children. This is not so *unless* the new husband formally adopts the children.

Often, the new husband voluntarily assumes the expenses of upbringing, but there remains a legal obligation on the first husband to continue to pay support. Of course, on remarriage of his ex-wife, his obligation to support her would almost certainly cease.

Even if you are not the natural parent of the child and have not adopted the child, you might still find yourself in a position where you have to support him or her. Under the Family Relations Act, if you and the child's parent were legally married and you contributed to the support and maintenance of the child for at least a year, you could be liable to pay ongoing support after your marriage terminated. If you and the child's parent were not married but lived together for at least two years and you contributed to the child's support and maintenance for at least one year, again a claim for child support could be made against you. The action for support would have to be brought within a year after the date you last contributed to the child's support.

Under the Divorce Act, you must support a child if you stand in place of a parent to the child. That means that you have acted as a parent toward the child and supported him or her in the past.

If the court has awarded custody of the children to the mother, the father is, in most cases, required to pay support. Even where custody is awarded to the father, the mother may be required to pay for their maintenance if she is financially able to do so.

The children are entitled to enjoy the same standard of living as they would have enjoyed if the parties had not separated. As far as possible, they should be saved from the hardship caused by a marital breakdown.

The payments awarded in a divorce are referred to as "maintenance." The amount of maintenance payments depends on many factors, among those being the costs of maintaining children, their necessary outstanding medical bills and projected medical expenses, the income of the father, the income of the mother, and the standard to which the children were used to and maintained at during the time when their parents were together.

In the average situation, assuming that your spouse is able to pay and you are not working, orders for children range between $100 and $500 per month. The older the child the more expensive his or her care and support is assumed to be.

You can get maintenance for children by proceeding in one of the following ways:

(a) Under the Family Relations Act, you can apply either to the provincial court or to the Supreme Court. Child support would continue to age 19 unless or until the child married or became self-supporting prior to that age.

(b) Under the Divorce Act, an order for child support can be incorporated into the divorce judgment. Support terminates at age 16 unless the child is still dependent. If the child is "unable by reason of illness, disability, or other cause to withdraw himself from (his parents') charge or to provide himself with the necessaries of life," then the maintenance can be continued. Continuing education is a common cause for dependency and there are cases where maintenance has been ordered to continue even past age 19.

i. HOW CAN I ENFORCE OR CHANGE A MAINTENANCE ORDER?

The enforcement and changing of a maintenance order for children is done in exactly the same way as enforcement or changing of an order for a spouse (see chapter 4).

Most parents do not mind paying support for their children but question whether the money is going to their benefit. They may be concerned that the custodial parent is using it for his or her own use and enjoyment. Unfortunately, there is very little that can be done. The court will not supervise the allocation of payments and very rarely will it order that the money be held in trust for the children until they are older. Child support is to cover the current expenses of caring for the children.

This does not mean that the money must go solely to buy food or clothing for the children or to pay for their activities. It goes into the "family pot" and is used to help make the mortgage payment, cover the hydro bills, etc., all of which benefit the child. Occasionally, a parent will be summonsed to court because he or she is in arrears on the support payments; the parent may argue that he or she is *not* in arrears because he or she gave money to the children directly or bought clothing or toys for them.While all of this might delight the children, it does not mean the child support payments have been satisfied. If this type of payment were allowed, the custodial parent would have to meet all the day-to-day expenses while the other parent gets to play Santa Claus.

j. HOW IS MAINTENANCE OF CHILDREN HANDLED IN SEPARATION AGREEMENTS?

If a separation agreement addresses maintenance of the children, a lot of problems and difficulty for both spouses can be avoided. Usually, the agreement is that one spouse will pay so much per month and the other spouse will not seek more than that in court. Such an agreement is legally binding to the extent that the amount may be collected by way of civil action or debt.

However, the courts have always taken the view that a parent cannot contract away the rights of the children to maintenance from the other parent. As a result, a provision of this nature in a separation agreement is not completely binding on either spouse as it affects the children, so an application to the court to vary the amount of maintenance set in the agreement may well be successful.

However, where there is such an agreement, the courts will look very closely at its terms when considering whether or not to allow a change in the amount of maintenance. If the party with custody of the children is seeking to increase the amount of maintenance, he or she will face great difficulties in convincing the judge that the amount should be increased from the level that was once acknowledged and accepted as satisfactory.

k. THE STATUS OF "ILLEGITIMATE" CHILDREN WITH RESPECT TO MAINTENANCE

The Family Relations Act requires a parent to pay support for a child up to the child's nineteenth birthday *regardless* of whether or not the spouses are living common-law or are married. In other words, the law regarding child support is the same whether or not the child is "legitimate." Until recently, applications for support for an "illegitimate" child were made under a separate statute called the Child Paternity and Support Act. That legislations has recently been repealed.

Note that in addition to child support, the mother can recover payment for expenses arising from and incidental to the following:

(a) prenatal care for herself or the child, or

(b) the birth of the child.

What if the man denies that he is he father of the child? If he is a step-father and the time limitation outlined on page 107 are met, it makes no difference that the child isn't "his." But if the relationship between the mother and her partner is more casual and they have not lived together for two years, then the man would only have to pay support if he was found by a judge to be the "real" father. This might require hearing evidence from witnesses to support the mother's story that she and the man were sleeping together about nine months before the birth of the child or that the man had referred to the child as "his." Alternatively, blood tests of the mother, child, and alleged father may be taken and introduced as evidence to show the percentage likelihood that the man is the father. The court does not have the jurisdiction to order someone to submit to a blood test, but it may draw an adverse inference if someone is asked to submit and refuses.

l. APART FROM MAINTENANCE, WHAT RESPONSIBILITIES DO PARENTS HAVE TOWARD THEIR CHILDREN?

Parents are entrusted with the care, custody, and control of children until they reach the age of majority. This is ancient law that reaches back beyond memory and has, until the last few centuries, been largely a matter of social custom. Today, there are basic rules and procedures set out in the law.

The parent/child relationship with its inherent duties and obligations supposedly continues until the age of majority (in British Columbia, age 19), but there is nothing the courts can practically do to enforce this. Whether parental control continues to age 19 is more a matter of fact, not law.

Beyond the age of 19, children are adults and on their own and the relationship in law between parents and children from that point on is essentially that of strangers even though they may continue to have close personal relationships.

Parents must maintain, protect, and nourish their children, and failure to do so is a criminal offence. To make the task of parents easier, it has always been the law that parents may use reasonable force in keeping their children in line and this is recognized in the Criminal Code. However, excessive force or abuse of children will bring rapid and severe punishment once the matter is brought before the courts. It may even result in the children being removed from the home and placed elsewhere.

m. WHAT RESPONSIBILITIES DO CHILDREN HAVE TOWARD THEIR PARENTS?

Under the Family Relations Act, a child over the age of 19 is liable to maintain and support a parent who is dependent by reason of age, illness, infirmity, or economic circumstances. Thus, the parent may make an application for support from a child in the same manner that a spouse would apply for support from a spouse. The same procedures for enforcement of such orders are available to parents and children as are available to spouses.

n. HOW DO I ADOPT A CHILD?

There are two ways to adopt a child in British Columbia: either privately or through the Superintendent of Family and Child Service. Anyone who wishes to adopt a child may apply directly to the Superintendent of Family and Child Service. Also, the local office of the Ministry of Social Services and Housing conducts such interviews and investigations as are advisable and completes all the necessary documents. In the case of agency adoptions, a lawyer's services are not usually required.

It should be pointed out, however, that because of the increasing use of contraceptives and availability of abortions, there are now very few unwanted newborn infants. Also, social attitudes are changing toward the single parent, so many previously unwanted children are being kept by their mothers. The result is a long waiting list, particularly for healthy Caucasian infants.

Couples who adopt usually do so because, for one reason or another, they cannot have children of their own. Because of the demand for children, single people or people living common-law have less chance of adopting the children in high demand.

In the case of a private adoption, unless the person applying to adopt is a blood relative of the child in question, the Superintendent of Family and Child Service will still be involved to the extent of investigating the home and reporting to the court the results of that investigation.

o. WHAT ABOUT ADOPTING MY SPOUSE'S CHILDREN OR ALLOWING MY SPOUSE TO ADOPT MY CHILDREN?

Unless the marriage has a good chance of being stable and long lasting, the time and expense expended in adopting the children will not justify the end result because, once the adoption goes through, both spouses are liable to maintain those children regardless of what happens.

You should also remember that the natural parents surrenders all rights to the child forever. This means that if the children are being supported by a former spouse, his or her obligation to support them will cease. So, if you have a steady income from this source, you should very carefully consider whether or not you wish to disrupt it by consenting to an adoption application. Under no circumstances should adoption of your spouse's children be undertaken merely in an attempt to cement the union and make it more permanent and durable. This is playing with the rights and future destiny of children merely to convenience the partners.

If you are seeking to adopt without consent, notice has to be given to the natural parent who will have the right to object. This can be a lengthy and complicated procedure. Whether the adoption succeeds depends entirely on the circumstances.

The court is most reluctant to dispense with a natural parent's consent to the adoption if he or she has any kind of relationship at all with the child. The court takes the position that the child has the right to know both parents and will sever that tie only in rare instances. Often the motivation behind a step-parent adoption is a desire to terminate the non-custodial parent's right to access. Recently, however, the courts have held that an adoption order does not end the natural parent's right to access if the access order has been made pursuant to the Divorce Act.

One party in a common-law union cannot adopt the children of the other. The couple must be legally married before a "step-parent adoption" can take place. The only way a common-law husband, for example, could adopt his "wife's" children would be for her to relinquish them for adoption, i.e., the children would then be legally the "husband's" but no longer the wife's! As to common-law spouses adopting unrelated children, they couldn't do so as a couple but one or the other could apply singly.

p. CHILDREN AND THE LAW

The children of today represent the society of tomorrow, and, to a very great extent, the quality of care and training our children receive determines the quality of our society in the years to come. For centuries the law did not really become involved with children or the family unless for some reason the family was disrupted and the children were somehow ejected out of a family situation to fend for themselves.

It is only within the last 50 years or so that the law has begun to take a more active role, but today there are statutes that give clear and ample power to the various government authorities to step into any situation for the purpose of protecting and maintaining children. The power is there, but in practice it is still only in very extreme cases that these agencies will actually intervene.

There are two reasons for this. First, there is tremendous public pressure placed upon the government to stay out of the personal lives of the citizens. This means that government agencies are very reticent about walking into a family situation unless there is a very clear and pressing need to do so.

Second, even when the authorities do step in on behalf of a child, the facilities the authorities have at their disposal to deal with the problem are very limited. However, things are changing in this regard and every month sees increasing resources and talent being brought to bear in the area of child protection.

Where children are involved in some form of legal dispute there is a great deal of emotionalism, and sometimes hysteria, involved. Disputes over children can be of the most difficult and complex nature both from a practical and legal point of view. Because of the complexities and problems involved and the importance of the outcome, this is not an area in which it is recommended that action be taken without competent legal counsel, experienced in this area.

Many people ask, "What are my legal duties toward my child?" Apart from the duties set out in the Family Relations Act, discussed in the earlier chapters of this book, the Criminal Code embodies certain specific duties.

DUTIES TENDING TO PRESERVATION OF LIFE

Duty of persons to provide necessaries -- Offence -- Punishment -- Presumptions

197. (1) Every one is under a legal duty

(a) as a parent, foster parent, guardian or head of a family, to provide necessaries of life for a child under the age of sixteen years;

(b) as a husband, to provide necessaries of life for his wife; and

(c) to provide necessaries of life to a person under his charge if that person

(i) is unable, by reason of detention, age, illness, insanity or other cause, to withdraw himself from that charge, and

(ii) is unable to provide himself with necessaries of life.

(2) Every one commits an offence who, being under a legal duty within the meaning of subsection (1), fails without lawful excuse, the proof of which lies upon him, to perform that duty, if

(a) with respect to a duty imposed by paragraph (1)(a) or (b),

(i) the person to whom the duty is owed is in destitute or necessitous circumstances, or

(ii) the failure to perform the duty endangers the life of the person to whom the duty is owed, or causes or is likely to cause the health of that person to be endangered permanently; or

(b) with respect to a duty imposed by paragraph (1)(c), the failure to perform the duty endangers the life of the person to whom the duty is owed, causes or is likely to cause the health of that person to be injured permanently.

Abandoning child

200. Every one who unlawfully abandons or exposes a child who is under the age of ten years, so that its life is or is likely to be endangered or its health is or is likely to be permanently injured, is guilty of an indictable offence and is liable to imprisonment for two years.

196. In this part

"abandon" or "expose" includes

(a) a wilful omission to take charge of a child by a person who is under a legal duty to do so, and

(b) dealing with a child in a manner that is likely to leave that child exposed to risk without protection;

"child" includes an adopted child and an illegitimate child;

"form of marriage" includes a ceremony of marriage that is recognized as valid

(a) by the law of the place where it was celebrated, or

(b) by the law of the place where an accused is tried, notwithstanding that it is not recognized as valid by the law of the place where it was celebrated;

"guardian" includes a person who has in law or in fact the custody or control of a child.

(2) Any person who, being the parent or guardian of the child and being able to do so, knowingly neglects to do that which would directly tend to prevent the child being or becoming a juvenile delinquent or to remove the conditions that render or are likely to render the child a juvenile delinquent is liable on summary conviction before a juvenile court or a magistrate to a fine not exceeding five hundred dollars or to imprisonment for a period not exceeding two years, or to both.

(3) The court or magistrate may postpone or adjourn the hearing of a charge under this section for such periods as the court may deem advisable or may postpone or adjourn the hearing sine die and may impose conditions upon any person found guilty under this section and suspend sentence subject to those conditions, and on proof at any time that those conditions have been violated may pass sentence on such person.

(4) It is not a valid defence to a prosecution under this section either that the child is of too tender years to understand or appreciate the nature or effect of the conduct of the accused, or that notwithstanding the

conduct of the accused the child did not in fact become a juvenile delinquent.

(5) Notwithstanding anything to the contrary in section 5 or in the provisions of the Criminal Code referred to in paragraph 5(1)(b), any prosecution for an offence under this section may be commenced within one year from the time when the offence is alleged to have been committed.

q. WHAT ROLE DOES THE GOVERNMENT TAKE?

As has been pointed out already, the Criminal Code offers a certain amount of protection to children in the sense of punishing the individuals failing to provide the necessaries of life to a child, abandoning a child, or contributing to a child's delinquency. The Family and Child Service Act is designed not to punish the offender but to protect the child.

This is often required not only where a child is being abused by the parents, but where the parents are unable to care for the child; where they are dead or missing; where the child has run away from home; or in any other situation in which a child is in need.

When a child has been apprehended (taken into the custody of the Superintendent of Family and Child Service), the Superintendent must present a written report to the court within seven days. At this time, a date will be fixed for a court hearing to determine whether or not the child is in need of protection. The parents or guardians must be given notice of this hearing and they have the right to be present, to be represented by a lawyer to speak for them, to cross-examine the witnesses, to call their own evidence, and to argue before the judge as to their feelings on what the outcome should be.

If the judge finds that the child is, in fact, in need of protection, he or she may make an order returning the child to the parents (but under the supervision of the social workers) or may order that the child remain in the care of the Superintendent of Family and Child Service either as a temporary ward or permanently.

Though there is a natural distrust of civil servants, experience has shown that the powers of the Superintendent of Family and Child Service are used wisely and often too sparingly. The agency never steps into an ordinary family situation where there is no trouble. The employees in that department are usually dedicated and concerned people who are willing to work out a solution without court action if at all possible. The power to seize a child is used only as a last resort or where the safety of the child is at stake.

Once the Superintendent has obtained an order for wardship of a child, he or she stands in the same position as that of the natural parent. Foster homes, group homes, and other facilities can be drawn upon for help as well as counselling, medical, and other professional help. Occasionally the child is returned immediately to the home from which he or she was apprehended and the wardship is used as a means of closely supervising the situation to ensure the child's safety and well being.

If there is a possibility of the child returning home shortly after the hearing, the Superintendent will often counsel and assist the parents in an attempt to get the situation resolved before the child actually returns to them. This is voluntary on their part, but unless there is co-operation, the return of the child may be delayed considerably.

Very often a citizen will see mistreatment of a child and wonder what to do. The law is that every citizen (including police officers, lawyers, and doctors), must report such incidents to the Superintendent of Family and Child Service immediately. A phone call to the local welfare office is the easiest way to do this.

Because of the nature of the agency, every complaint of maltreatment received is investigated. If you are contacted by this agency concerning your child, you should not take offence or immediately assume that the department feels that you are abusing your child. First, it is as concerned about the welfare of your child as you are and, second, the report may have been totally false or misleading, in which case the agency will be the first to drop the matter.

There are too many children in need of its services for it to spend its time harassing the public. It is suggested that you co-operate in every way with the representative who contacts you because without doubt you are both engaged in the same pursuit — the welfare of your child. However, should it appear that the matter is not going to be terminated immediately and that there may be an on-going investigation, you would be wise to consult immediately with a lawyer.

r. WHAT RIGHTS DO CHILDREN HAVE BEFORE THE LAW?

We have seen that there are laws requiring that children be supported, fed, and nourished. Failing this, there are certain branches of the government that have the right to step in on behalf of children.

The rights of children to enter into contracts, to marry, and to generally deal in public affairs are severely limited by the law. We have already seen the restrictions on children marrying and the consent that they require.

Children generally are not allowed to enter into contracts and, should they do so, are entitled to repudiate (cancel) the contracts when they reach their adult age (19). The one exception to this is where a child enters into a contract for "necessaries" which have frequently been deemed to include cars and other major purchases. The law in this area can become somewhat complicated.

Generally, the problems with children's rights tend to arise in family and criminal law disputes. As we shall see later, children may be prosecuted criminally — in a special way — and great disputes rage as to whether or not, because of the informality of the proceedings, their legal rights are protected.

A husband and wife who are splitting up must decide the issues of custody of and maintenance for the children. Frequently, children get classed along the same lines as property and money. This "bartering away" of children's rights is tempered somewhat by the family advocate who is empowered to appear in court on behalf of the children to be sure that their best interests are represented. (But see section **d.** of this chapter regarding the current restraint on family advocate appointments.)

s. HOW ARE CHILDREN PROSECUTED UNDER THE CRIMINAL LAW?

In Canada, children under the age of 17 cannot be prosecuted for criminal acts directly. They are, instead, prosecuted by procedures under the Young Offenders Act, which has tried to strike a balance between the needs of young people and the interests of society. The act contains a Declaration of Principle stating that society must be protected from the illegal behavior of young persons and thus they are to be held responsible for their acts. Because of this, the young person is to be afforded all of the protection an adult receives in our criminal justice system.

The declaration goes on to acknowledge that in view of their level of development, however, young persons will not in all instances be held as accountable for their behavior as adults. An example of the lesser degree of accountability is reflected in the dispositions available under the act. When an offence is committed — criminal, motor vehicle, liquor, or certain others — the police carry on their investigation in much the same manner as in any other case. However, once it is determined that a young person is involved, the procedure becomes markedly different. The police send a report to the prosecutor who reviews it to see whether a charge is proper, that is, whether the circumstances support a charge and whether there's sufficient evidence to prove it.

Once that stage is passed, the prosecutor then considers the youth who has committed the offence. If it is a person who has not been in trouble before, and if the offence is a fairly minor one, the prosecutor will likely write to the youth's parents, outline the circumstances, and leave it to them to take proper disciplinary action. If the charge is more serious, the prosecutor may refer the matter to a probation officer to carry out a pre-court inquiry. The probation officer contacts the youth and the family and recommends that —

(a) the matter proceed to court,

(b) there be no further action, or

(c) the youth be diverted (i.e., dealt with outside the formal court setting).

For this last alternative to be used, the young person must acknowledge responsibility for the offence, otherwise the case must be dealt with in court. The alternative measures suggested by the probation officer might include such things as writing an essay, restitution, community service work, or some form of counselling. There will be no formal record of a conviction. The final decision rests with the prosecutor.

If the youth already has a record, or if the charges are a serious concern in the community, no pre-court inquiry is conducted and the matter proceeds directly to court.

If there is to be court action, a summons is delivered to the parents as well as the youth, and a parent must attend court to prove the youth's age. The young person must have been over 12 and under 18 at the time the offence was committed. At the first appearance, the judge asks the young person if he or she has talked to a lawyer. Normally, there is duty

125

counsel present to speak to the youth and advise him or her what to do at this early stage. If the youth asks the judge to appoint a lawyer for him or her, the judge *must* do so and there is no cost to the accused or his or her family. The matter is then generally adjourned several weeks to allow time for this appointment to be made and for the lawyer to learn the particulars of the alleged offence. On the next court date, if the youth pleads guilty, the prosecutor relates the circumstances to the judge. The judge almost always asks for a report from the probation officer before sentencing the offender. This pre-sentence report outlines the youth's background, education, home life, criminal record, and so on. With this information, the judge decides the sentence that would best benefit the child and the interests of society.

If the youth pleads not guilty, the case is adjourned for a trial at which point he prosecutor calls evidence to prove the allegations beyond a reasonable doubt as in any adult case.

t. WHAT CAN THE YOUTH COURT DO TO A YOUTH WHO IS FOUND GUILTY?

The Young Offenders Act tries to balance the young person's needs with the public interest and emphasizes the protection of the public. There is a wide range of dispositions available:

(a) The least that can happen is an absolute discharge, which means that there is no record of the conviction.

(b) A fine not exceeding $1 000 may be imposed.

(c) The youth can be ordered to pay an amount to the victim of the offence as compensation for loss of or damage to property, loss of income or support, or for special damages for personal injury arising from the offence where the value can be easily determined.

(d) There can be an order that property be returned to the victim or that the youth compensate the victim by way of personal services.

(e) The young person can be required to perform community service (e.g., doing volunteer work for a community group, visiting a senior citizens' home or perhaps cleaning up a park area). The maximum number of hours that may be assigned is 240.

(f) The young person may be detained for treatment if it appears he or she is suffering from a physical or mental illness or disorder, a psychological disorder, an emotional disturbance, a learning disability or mental retardation.

(g) A period of probation may be imposed for up to two years.

(h) Most seriously, the youth may be detained in custody for up to two years (or if the offence committed is one where an adult could receive a life sentence, the youth can be detained for up to three years). If this sentence is imposed, the judge must specify whether the youth is to be held in secure custody or open custody. The act has specific criteria that must be met before the former can be imposed. Open custody includes a community residential centre, group home, wilderness camp, and similar facilities.

(i) The court can impose whatever other reasonable conditions seems advisable in the best interests of the young person and the public.

If parents are having problems with their child, they may ask the judge to impose special additional terms to the probation such as curfew, not associating with certain people or going certain places, etc. Attempt to discuss the matter first with the probation officer, but if this is not possible then it should be suggested to the judge at the time of sentencing. When sentencing is taking place, step forward and wait until the judge recognizes you and asks you to speak; then express your concerns. Usually you will be asked in any event if you wish to say anything and that is the time to raise these matters.

If the offence charged is serious enough, or if the youth's behavior in general is such that it is in the interests of the youth and of society that he or she be dealt with in adult court, the prosecutor may bring an application to have the youth transferred there. If the application is successful, the youth will then have to face the same charge as if he or she were an adult and be subject to the same penalties that an adult would face.

This usually happens when the youth is a constant problem and has a record of repeated offences and warnings and the remedies of the court are simply not working. This is a serious matter, and the application will be made on one of the first appearances of the youth on the charge. The prosecutor will inform the judge of the intention to make the application, and a date will be set.

In considering such an application, the judge must take into account the following:

(a) The seriousness of the alleged offence and the circumstances in which it was allegedly committed

(b) The age, maturity, character, and background of the young person and the record of past convictions

(c) How the legislation will differ if the youth is transferred. Here a major consideration will usually be the limitations on how long a young person can be held in custody under the Young Offenders Act. If it's felt that more than two or three years in a correctional system is required, transfer is necessary.

(d) A comparison of the resources in the juvenile and adult systems. The court may recognize that a young person may have exhausted the resources available in the juvenile system.

u. CAN THE YOUTH COURT BLAME PARENTS FOR THEIR CHILD'S OFFENCE?

The Young Offenders Act recognizes that parents are responsible for the care and supervision of their children but this concept does not extend to vicarious liability. Parents cannot be ordered to pay a fine, damages, or costs when a child is found guilty of an offence.

v. WHERE CAN I TURN FOR HELP CONTROLLING MY CHILD?

Frequently parents find themselves in the situation of having a child under 19 who is beyond their control. The solution may well require the involvement of all family members in counselling, or a mental health professional may be required if the problem stems from a mental disorder. Drugs and/or alcohol abuse may be involved and, again, there are resources available to deal with the addicted child.

Our advice is to contact the Ministry of Social Services and Housing who can advise you of the various individuals or agencies available. If your problem is extreme, the Superintendent of Family and Child Service may even step in as a temporary guardian to the child — either by way of a short-term care agreement or a court order for temporary wardship.

6
PROPERTY DISPUTES

a. CAN A MARRIED WOMAN OWN PROPERTY?

Prior to the 19th century, the law considered that a woman's legal personality merged her husband's when she married. Therefore, on her marriage, all her property became her husband's.

In the late 19th century, the Married Woman's Property Act was passed. This act gave a married woman the capacity to purchase, own, and deal with real or personal property as if she were single. To protect her separate property, a woman was also given the right to sue in her own name.

b. WHO OWNS WHAT IN A COMMON-LAW MARRIAGE?

In section **d.** below, the family assets approach in the Family Relations Act is discussed. This is the presumption that each spouse has an equal interest in property ordinarily used for a family purpose. This approach does not apply to a common-law marriage, the parties' legal position is much more unsettled.

If property is jointly acquired and put into the names of both parties, there should be no dispute over the fact that each is entitled to a half interest. But what if the property was acquired by only one party (perhaps before the common-law relationship even began) and then either the whole or a half interest is given to the other party?

Generally, the law says that a gift between common-law spouses is permanent and irrevocable. This presumption can be rebutted by clear evidence to the contrary, but in most cases this evidence is not forthcoming because oral evidence alone is generally very weak and conflicting. The simple rule is that you are presumed to have the intention that would be the natural intention behind your act. For example, if you make an apparently outright gift to someone, you are presumed at law to have intended to make an outright gift. As you must incur a great deal of trouble and expense to rebut this presumption be careful when making gifts to a common-law spouse.

What is much more common, and much more complex to determine, is a situation in which the parties jointly acquire property but it is put into the name of one party alone, or a situation where one party owns property alone but the other spends untold hours working on the property and improving its value.

As the number of common-law relationships increases, so do the number of property disputes of this kind. If one spouse can persuade the court that there was a common intention that the property belong to both spouses, the court will find that the property-owning spouse actually holds a certain portion of the property "in trust" for the other and that the one party is entitled to be paid for this interest. Those cases are rare. In most instances the "common intention" can't be proved.

However, there is still a remedy open to the party who doesn't own the property. If he or she can show the court that the other has been "unjustly enriched" at his or her expense, then again the court may find the existence of a trust. For example, the common-law wife on a farm is a familiar situation. Her common-law husband owned the farm before he met her. She moved to the farm and worked diligently over many years raising animals, helping with the haying, etc. Then the relationship ended and the "husband" said "Sorry, dear, the farm is mine."

If the court hears from witnesses who knew that the husband regularly referred to the farm as "ours" and had promised his "wife" that she would be rewarded for her efforts by sharing in the farm, that common interest would be present and the husband would be found to own a portion of the farm as trustee for the wife. If this isn't the case, the court may find that the husband benefitted at the wife's expense and, again, would find that he owns a portion of the farm as trustee for her.

It's a complicated and expensive matter to argue about in court. So the best advice to a common-law spouse is to get your name on the title.

c. WHAT IS THE DIFFERENCE BETWEEN OWNERSHIP AND POSSESSION OF PROPERTY?

Ownership means a right in the legal title to the property itself; possession means a right to use or occupy the property. This distinction is important because the law treats ownership disputes between husband and wife differently from possession disputes. In other words, a wife may not "own" the family home, but normally she does have a strong claim of possession. The procedure for the adjudication of either of these disputes is set out in the Family Relations Act.

d. THE FAMILY ASSETS APPROACH

Before the Family Relations Act of 1978, a very complicated set of legal rules and principles that applied to the division of property between married people led to a great deal of uncertainty and lengthy and protracted litigation. In many cases, the husband would end up with most of the property because he was usually out in the work force earning money and accumulating assets. In many cases, the wife was simply out of luck. The best she could hope for was some reasonable amount of support from her husband.

The legislature considered numerous ways of dividing matrimonial property between married people and eventually decided on the family assets approach. This concept gives effect to the premise that a family should be treated as one economic unit, and it gives a great deal of flexibility in terms of assets that are known as non-family assets.

A family asset is defined in section 45(2) of the Family Relations Act as "Property owned by one or both spouses and ordinarily used by a spouse or a minor child of either spouse for a family purpose." Therefore, the family car, the bank account that is used for household purposes, the boat, the cottage, and the house are all family assets. So, too, are such items as pensions and registered retirement savings plans.

Even property used primarily for your spouse's business purposes may be classed as a family asset if it can be shown that you made a contribution to the acquisition of the property or the operation of the business; and the act makes it clear that fulfilling the role of a homemaker constitutes a contribution.

Upon separation or divorce, either spouse is entitled to go to the court and ask for an equal division of the family assets. Normally, the court distributes these assets equally. To prevent injustices in some specific cases, the court has jurisdiction to make an unequal division of family assets in certain circumstances.

If you have entered into a marriage agreement setting out the division of family assets, that will be considered. If you have lived together for only a short time, equality of economic status may result in injustice. Therefore, the court will take into account how long you lived together while married.

It will also take into account how long you have been separated. The date when the property was acquired will be of interest to the court. If one of you acquired property by gift or inheritance from some third party, that spouse will likely be entitled to the property, even though it is a family asset. In addition, the court may take into account any other relevant circumstances relating to the property or how it was used or how it was maintained or acquired.

Only the Supreme Court of British Columbia has jurisdiction to deal with these types of issues. The family court has no jurisdiction.

Your spouse cannot defeat your claim by putting a piece of property in the name of a corporation. For example, if the husband owns shares in a corporation that owns the family home, his shares in the corporation form part of the family assets and they are subject to equal division. If your spouse threatens to get rid of some of the property that has been in his or her name during the marriage in order to prevent a fair and equal division upon separation or divorce, the court may make an order restraining such disposition.

The court has very wide powers of discretion in deciding what to do with family assets. It can order the re-allocation and transfer of specified property; it can order the sale of any property and the division of the proceeds; it can charge any property with any obligation imposed by its order; it can order one spouse to pay the other a sum of money in order to make a property adjustment in family assets.

Only people that are married to one another or who have been divorced less than two years can take this approach. Common-law spouses or people who have been divorced more than two years cannot avail themselves of these provisions of the Family Relations Act.

e. OWNERSHIP OF THE MATRIMONIAL HOME

1. What is joint tenancy?

Couples who purchase a home for themselves and their family often have the legal title placed in joint tenancy. Title in this form involves two important legal implications:

(a) If either spouse dies, title to the entire property legally passes "automatically" to the survivor without forming part of the estate of the deceased. This is known as the right to survivorship.

(b) If the spouses sell the property, each is entitled to receive one-half of the net proceeds of the sale because each spouse owns one-half of the house.

2. Who owns the home if legal title is in the name of one spouse only?

Under the Family Relations Act, any property that has been ordinarily used for family purposes becomes a family asset. Obviously, this includes the matrimonial home. As discussed earlier, as a family asset, the home will almost without exception be split 50/50 between the spouses at the time of separation or divorce regardless of whose name the property is registered in and regardless of who contributed the most financially to the purchase of the property.

It is possible to "contract out" of this division if you and your spouse agree that an equal division isn't what you want. The act allows you to enter into an agreement dealing with how property is to be owned, managed, or divided. If the property is registered in the name of your spouse only and you have concerns that the property may be sold or mortgaged without your approval (or without your knowledge!), it is possible to register your agreement in the Land Title Office. This effectively stops the property in question from being dealt with in any way without your consent.

Another safeguard that is open to wives only is filing a lien under the Land (Spouse Protection) Act. This amounts to swearing an affidavit that the property in question has been the residence of you and your husband within the last year. The affidavit and various accompanying documents are filed in the Land Title Office and, again, this is sufficient to restrict your husband from dealing with the property in any way without your consent.

135

f. POSSESSION OF THE MATRIMONIAL HOME

Each spouse is equally entitled to be in possession of the matrimonial home unless the parties themselves have reached an agreement to the contrary and embodied this in an agreement or unless the court orders otherwise. The provincial court (family court) cannot make such an order. You must apply to the Supreme Court for an order excluding one spouse from the premises.

A dispute over possession of the property is almost always decided in favor of the spouse who has custody of the children. If there are no kids, the court seems to look at how intolerable one spouse is making life for the other. Such an order is for temporary relief only — just pending determination of the rights to the property.

As previously mentioned, this determination of rights doesn't necessarily mean that the property must immediately be sold. The court may find the spouses entitled to an equal division of the new equity in the property yet postpone any sale until such time as the children are finished school, for example. So the temporary right to exclusive possession may, in fact, continue for some years.

Although each party is entitled to an equal division of the contents of the home, since they are family assets, the court may postpone such division and permit the person who occupies the home to continue to have the use of some or all of the contents. Frequently, the court decides who is responsible for repairing and maintaining the home and paying the mortgage payments, hydro payments, water payments, and all other expenses of living in a home.

g. WOMEN'S RIGHTS TO CONTRACT AND INCUR DEBTS

According to law, women are on an equal footing with men as far as their rights to borrow money and enter into contracts are concerned. However, this is of little practical value because, as a matter of practice, it may be difficult for a married woman to find an institution that will lend her money in her name alone unless she has adequate security. This business policy renders her legal right to borrow money rather useless.

The reasons evolve from history and experience. Women, according to history, are poor credit risks because they have more difficulty finding employment, tend to hold lower paying jobs, and are frequently prevented from obtaining work because of their children. Although this may not be their fault and although the result be very unjust, it is a fact of life.

It is a very difficult thing for a woman to get on her feet financially once she is separated from her husband, especially if she has children to raise. Financial institutions take all this into consideration but adequate counselling in financial matters is very difficult to get. Resources that you can turn to, however, are bankers and some lawyers. You may also refer to *Credit, Debt, and Bankruptcy*, another publication in the Self-Counsel Legal Series, for useful advice.

Debts that have been incurred by the husband and co-signed by the wife are the equal responsibility of both. However, when either party does contract a debt after the separation, and in his or her own name, it does not affect the other.

The one exception to this is an old common-law doctrine that a wife may charge her husband's credit for necessaries. Although a husband had no obligation to support his wife, he did have an obligation to supply her with the necessaries of life, and if he failed to do so, she could go to any merchant and obtain food and clothing and have him bill her husband who could be compelled by the courts to pay. This was a beautiful remedy in theory, but, of course, very few merchants are happy to get involved in such disputes and again the law and the practice are widely divergent. Consequently, this right has dimmed considerably in importance and is very difficult to enforce.

Of course, if the husband and wife have joint credit cards, there is joint liability as long as those accounts remain open and neither party has cancelled them. In this case there would be joint liability with both parties being responsible for payment of the bills.

h. THEFT BETWEEN SPOUSES

It is often thought that a husband and wife cannot be charged with stealing from each other, but this is not strictly the case. Where a marriage is on the rocks, it is possible that one can be charged with stealing from the other as section 289 of the Criminal Code makes most clear.

> 289. (1) Subject to subsection (2), no husband or wife, during cohabitation, commits theft of anything that is by law the property of the other.
>
> (2) A husband or wife commits theft who, intending to desert or on deserting the other or while living apart from the other, fraudulently takes or converts anything that is by law the property of the other in a manner that, if it were done by another person, would be theft.
>
> (3) Every one commits theft who, during cohabitation of a husband and wife, knowingly
>
>> (a) assists either of them in dealing with anything that is by law the property of the other in a manner that would be theft if they were not married, or
>>
>> (b) receives from either of them anything that is by law the property of the other and has been obtained from the other by dealing with it in a manner that would be theft if they were not married.

This section is rarely, if ever, used because of the difficulties involved in proving the theft. However, it is possible for a charge to be laid and prosecuted by the Crown. If a spouse feels particularly vindictive, such a charge may be laid even though there is little chance of its being successful. Reason does not always prevail in these situations, and the spouse making the complaint may see some value in the nuisance factor involved in such a charge, if nothing else.

7
LAWYERS AND LEGAL AID

a. LAWYERS

1. How to choose a lawyer

There is no secret method for choosing a good lawyer — no more so than choosing a professional person in any other field such as medicine, accounting, auto mechanics, or plumbing.

Ask your friends and relatives if they can recommend anyone — or warn you away from anyone. But keep in mind that just because your brother's lawyer is good at conveyancing, it does not follow that he or she will be good in family law matters. There are so many areas of law that most lawyers specialize to a certain degree.

If you cannot get a recommendation and you live in any of the major centres in British Columbia, you have available to you a Lawyer Referral Service (listed under that heading in the phone book). If you call them and request a lawyer experienced in family law, they will make an appropriate referral. You are entitled to one half-hour of consultation for a fee of $10. Past that point you are charged at the lawyer's regular rate. By that time you should be able to tell whether you would like the particular lawyer to act for you. Don't be afraid to discuss the fee; it's perfectly acceptable to shop around.

2. Be prepared

Before you see your lawyer, prepare yourself, in writing. Write out your name, address, age, place of birth, children's names, and the names of all the other people involved in your problem with as much information about them, their work, and living situations as you can. Then write out a brief history of your problem, how it came about, what happened, and what you want done. The lawyer will want to know details about your financial circumstances and that of your spouse. Put some thought into it, so that when you go to see your lawyer you can hand over the sheet. In this way you will also have in your own mind a fresh and clear picture of the situation.

Do not go to see your lawyer without any idea of what you want, or of who is involved, or without all of the documents and information. You will only be told to go away and come back when you have it all together. Every minute is costing you. Don't waste time and then blame the lawyer because the bill is high. Whether your lawyer gets anything done or not, you are paying for his or her time.

3. How much will it cost?

A lawyer has nothing to sell but time. He or she has no other product. Accordingly, the fee will reflect the amount of time, whether on the telephone, in the office, or over lunch, that your case consumes. Should you call him or her at home, expect very high billings for that. Of course, if you want to keep your lawyer working for you, call him or her at home only in the most extreme emergencies. Everything that you do to save time, everything that you can do for yourself, will keep your bill down.

Frequently lawyers are not prepared to wait to bill you until the whole case is completed. As previously stated the case can take a long time until it is fully disposed of. As a result, lawyers will often send interim bills as the matter progresses. Feel free to discuss this with your lawyer before deciding to retain him or her.

If there is a dispute involved — with a spouse, for example, over children, property, etc. — it may not be possible for your lawyer to pinpoint exactly how much the bill will be because it is impossible to say how much time will be involved. It will depend on how the dispute goes, what the other side does, and what difficulties arise. In that case, you should ask for an estimate based on an hourly rate.

Virtually all lawyers have been stung by clients who do not pay. The solution is to get the fee in advance (usually called a retainer). It is usually not the full fee but a good portion of it. It is held in a special account, called the trust account, and used only for items such as court fees that must be paid for on your behalf. The lawyer can use it only if he or she sends a bill to you setting out the details of the account. When you deliver the retainer, get a receipt.

Often the person seeking help has no cash. Some lawyers accept property as a retainer, and others work with little or no retainer. If you are seeking help and you have a house in joint tenancy or a spouse who would be able to afford court costs that might be awarded, it is often possible to get the lawyer to act if you turn over these proceeds at a later date. Talk to your lawyer about it.

Initially your lawyer should try to get your spouse to pay for the costs of the proceedings. These costs include a portion of your legal fees. It's common for a court to award the wife her costs, but the husband rarely is awarded his.

b. GOVERNMENT APPOINTED LAWYERS

The provincial government provides counsel in certain matters before the family court under these circumstances:

(a) If one party is being charged with a criminal offence or with an offence under the Family Relations Act (for disobeying a custody or access order, for example), Crown counsel will prosecute the case and hiring a private lawyer is not necessary.

(b) If the applicant has custody of a child and there has been violence of a "reasonable apprehension of violence," counsel will be provided until a final order is obtained.

(c) If the applicant is receiving social assistance, counsel will be provided to make an application for maintenance.

(d) If an order for maintenance has been made and is not being obeyed, counsel will be provided to enforce proceedings if the order has been registered with the Family Maintenance Enforcement Program.

c. LEGAL AID

The legal aid system in British Columbia, although supported by the provincial government, is not a government program with unlimited funds to assist people with legal problems. Because of the limited funds, there are restrictions on the type of matters legal aid will pursue.

There are two tests to determine eligibility. The first is a "means" test. The test varies depending on the density of the population where the client lives. In Vancouver and Lower Mainland, a person is eligible if his or her income is at or blow the scale set out below:

Number in family	Maximum monthly net income to qualify
1	$ 840
2	$1 180
3	$1 500
4	$1 700
5	$1 960
6	$2 100
7	$2 270

In the more sparsely populated areas, the maximum monthly net include to qualify is considerably less. For example, in a rural area, a family of one would not qualify for legal aid unless his or her monthly net income was under $660.

The second hurdle is that the family matter for which you want representation must be urgent. Guidelines are set forth to help determine whether or not a matter falls within this category:

(a) Does the client appear to be emotionally disturbed, or is there a language deficiency or other factor that would make self-representation impossible?

(b) Is the client or a child subject to physical abuse?

(c) Is custody contested and have the parties tried conciliation to resolve this issue without success? (**Note:** if the applicant does not have custody, if there has not been abuse, and if the situation with the custodial parent appears to be stable, the matter will not be considered urgent.)

(d) Is access in serious dispute, for example, is the custodial parent refusing or threatening to refuse any further access? (Again, whether or not the parties have sought resolution through conciliation is a factor.)

(e) Is there a danger that a child may be removed from the jurisdiction?

(f) Do serious immigration implications arise from the matrimonial dispute?

(g) Is there a possibility that entitlement to maintenance may be lost?

(h) Without legal representation, is it likely the applicant's financial situation will worsen? For example, is the respondent refusing to disclose assets or are serious attempts at enforcing payment of maintenance proving unsuccessful?

Residents of the Greater Vancouver area can apply at the legal aid office, 191 Alexander Street, Vancouver. In other areas, residents should apply to the legal aid clinics operated by the Legal Services Society office of that area.

CANADIAN
ORDER FORM
SELF-COUNSEL SERIES

01/89

NATIONAL TITLES

____	Upper Left-Hand Corner	10.95
____	Wise and Healthy Living	
____	Working Couples	5.50
____	Write Right!	5.50

PROVINCIAL TITLES

Divorce Guide
❏ B.C. 9.95 ❏ Alberta 9.95 ❏ Saskatchewan 12.95
❏ Manitoba 11.95 ❏ Ontario 12.95

Employer/Employee Rights
❏ B.C. 7.95 ❏ Alberta 6.95 ❏ Ontario 6.95

Incorporation Guide
❏ B.C. 14.95 ❏ Alberta 14.95 ❏ Manitoba/Saskatchewan 12.95 ❏ Ontario 14.95

Landlord/Tenant Rights
❏ B.C. 7.95 ❏ Alberta 6.95 ❏ Ontario 7.95

Marriage & Family Law
❏ B.C. 7.95 ❏ Alberta 8.95 ❏ Ontario 7.95

Probate Guide
❏ B.C. 12.95 ❏ Alberta 10.95 ❏ Ontario 11.95

Real Estate Guide
❏ B.C. 8.95 ❏ Alberta 7.95 ❏ Ontario 8.50

Small Claims Court Guide
❏ B.C. 7.95 ❏ Alberta 7.50 ❏ Ontario 7.50

Wills
❏ B.C. 6.50 ❏ Alberta 6.50 ❏ Ontario 5.95
❏ Wills/Probate Procedure for Manitoba/Saskatchewan 5.95

PACKAGED FORMS

Divorce Forms
❏ B.C 11.95 ❏ Alberta 10.95 ❏ Saskatchewan 12.95
❏ Manitoba 10.95 ❏ Ontario 14.95

Incorporation
❏ B.C 14.95 ❏ Alberta 14.95 ❏ Saskatchewan 14.95
❏ Manitoba 14.95 ❏ Ontario 14.95 ❏ Federal 7.95
❏ Minute Books 17.95
❏ Power of Attorney Kit 9.95

Probate
❏ B.C. Administration 14.95 ❏ B.C. Probate 14.95
❏ Alberta 14.95 ❏ Ontario 15.50
❏ Rental Form Kit (B.C., Alberta, Saskatchewan, Ontario) 4.95
❏ Have You Made Your Will? 5.95
❏ If You Love Me Put It In Writing – Contract Kit 14.95
❏ If You Leave Me Put It In Writing – B.C. Separation
 Agreement Kit 14.95

Interim Agreement
❏ B.C. 2.50 ❏ Alberta 2.50 ❏ Ontario 2.50

Note: All prices subject to change without notice.

Books are available in book and department stores, or use the order form below. Please enclose cheque or money order (plus sales tax where applicable) or give us your MasterCard or Visa number (please include validation and expiry dates).

✂ ....

(PLEASE PRINT)

Name _____

Address _____

City _____ Province _____

Postal Code _____

❏ Visa/ ❏ MasterCard Number_____

Validation Date_____ Expiry Date _____

If order is under $20.00, add $1.00 for postage and handling.
Please send orders to:

SELF-COUNSEL PRESS

1481 Charlotte Road

North Vancouver, British Columbia   V7J 1H1

❏ Check here for free catalogue.